AF083870

Landscapes of
TENERIFE

a countryside guide
Eleventh edition

Noel Rochford
*revised by Sunflower Books
with Conny Spelbrink and Jan Kostura*

SUNFLOWER BOOKS

Eleventh edition © 2025
Sunflower Books™
PO Box 36160
London SW7 3WS, UK
www.sunflowerbooks.co.uk

All rights reserved. No part of this publication may be reproduced, stored in a retrieval system, or transmitted by any form or by any means, electronic, mechanical, photocopying, recording or otherwise, without the prior written permission of the publishers.

Sunflower Books and 'Landscapes' are Registered Trademarks

ISBN 978-1-85691-562-5

Taginaste rojo ('Pride of Tenerife')

Important note to the reader

We have tried to ensure that the descriptions and maps in this book are error-free at press date. The book will be updated, where necessary, in future editions. It will be very helpful for us to receive your comments (sent to info@sunflowerbooks.co.uk, please) for the updating of future editions.

We also rely on those who use this book — especially walkers — to take along a good supply of common sense when they explore. Conditions change fairly rapidly on Tenerife, and *storm damage or bulldozing may make a route unsafe at any time*. If the route is not as we outline it here, and your way ahead is not secure, return to the point of departure. *Never attempt to complete a tour or walk under hazardous conditions!* Please read carefully the notes on pages 40-49, and the introductory comments at the beginning of each tour and walk (road conditions, equipment, grade, distances, time). Explore *safely*, and at the same time respect the beauty of the countryside.

Cover photograph: Masca (Car tour 3)
Title page: candelabra spurge (Euphorbia canariensis)

Photos: R Lefever: 16, 31, 44, 57, 62, 71, 101, 142; Shutterstock: 2, 6-7, 14-5, 18, 21, 24-5, 26-7, 29, 32, 32-3, 35, 36-7, 38-9, 42-3, 54-5, 58-9, 66, 81, 84-5, 87, 88-9, 90, 92-3, 99 (top), 104, 106 (top), 110-1, 112-3, 114, 116-7, 124, 130-1, 136, 144, 146, 148, 153, 156; C Spelbrink: 125 (top); A Stieglitz: 22-3, 28, 34-5, 50-1, 67, 80, 107, 133, 134, 150-1; P Underwood: 1, 31, 41, 61 (top), 62, 63, 80-1, 96, 106; all others: the author
Maps: Nick Hill for Sunflower Books. Base map data © OpenStreetMap contributors. Contour data made available under ODbL (opendatacommons.org/licenses/odbl/1.0)
Drawings: Sharon Rochford
A CIP catalogue record for this book is available from the British Library.
Printed and bound in England: Short Run Press, Exeter

Contents

Preface	5
Publisher's Note; Acknowledgements; Useful books	6
Getting about	7
Plans of Puerto de la Cruz and Santa Cruz showing city exits and bus departure points	8
Picnics and short walks	10
Picnic/short walk suggestions	11
Touring	19
THE OROTAVA VALLEY AND LAS CAÑADAS (TOUR 1) Puerto de la Cruz • La Orotava • Las Cañadas • Los Gigantes • Guía de Isora • Adeje • Playa de las Américas • Playa de los Cristianos • Vilaflor • Las Cañadas • Puerto de la Cruz	20
THE RUGGED ANAGA PENINSULA (TOUR 2) Puerto de la Cruz • Cruz del Carmen • Pico del Inglés • Roque Negro • El Bailadero • Chamorga • Taganana • Almáciga • Benijo • San Andrés • Igueste • Puerto de la Cruz	25
SPECTACULAR NORTHWEST SETTINGS (TOUR 3) Puerto de la Cruz • San Juan de la Rambla • Icod de los Vinos • Garachico • Punta de Teno • Teno Alto • Santiago del Teide • Icod el Alto • Puerto de la Cruz	29
QUIET CORNERS OF THE ANAGA (TOUR 4) Puerto de la Cruz • Tacoronte • Bajamar • Punta del Hidalgo • Batán • Las Carboneras • Taborno • Pico del Inglés • La Laguna • Puerto de la Cruz	34
THE SUN-BAKED SOUTH (TOUR 5) Puerto de la Cruz • La Laguna • La Esperanza • El Portillo • Güímar • Arico • Candelaria • Puerto de la Cruz	37
Walking	40
Grading, waymarking, maps, GPS	40
Where to stay	42
Weather	43
Nuisances	45
What to take	46
Country code	46
Advice for walkers	47
Spanish for walkers	48
Organisation of the walks	49

4 Landscapes of Tenerife (Cañadas • Orotava • Teno • Anaga)

THE OROTAVA VALLEY AND LAS CAÑADAS

- 1 Two coastal walks from Puerto de la Cruz — 50
- 2 Aguamansa to Chasna — 56
- 3 Aguamansa • La Caldera • Choza Chimoche • Lomo de los Brezos • Aguamansa — 59
- 4 Aguamansa • Pinolere • La Florida — 62
- 5 La Caldera • Choza El Topo • Choza Almadi • Pino Alto • La Florida — 64
- 6 The Organos 'high road': La Caldera • Lomo de los Brezos • Aguamansa — 69
- 7 The Candelaria Trail: La Caldera • La Crucita • Arafo — 72
- 8 El Portillo • Corral del Niño • Choza Chimoche • La Caldera — 76
- 9 Las Cañadas — 79
- 10 El Teide — 84
- 11 Roques de García and La Catedral — 88
- 12 Montaña de Guajara — 91
- 13 El Portillo • Piedra de los Pastores • Galería La Zarza • Chanajiga • Palo Blanco — 94

THE NORTHWEST

- 14 Icod el Alto • La Corona • Chanajiga • Palo Blanco — 97
- 15 Icod el Alto • El Lagar • La Guancha — 100
- 16 La Montañeta • Las Arenas Negras • Los Partidos de Franquis • Erjos • Los Silos — 107
- 17 Erjos • Las Lagunetas • El Palmar — 112
- 18 Restaurante Fleytas • Montaña Jala • Los Bolicos • Degollada de la Mesa • Restaurante Fleytas — 115
- 19 La Tabaiba • Teno Alto • Buenavista — 119
- 20 La Montañeta (El Palmar) • Teno Alto • Teno Bajo • (Faro de Teno) • Buenavista — 122
- 21 Los Silos • Talavera • Los Silos — 126

THE ANAGA PENINSULA

- 22 Punta del Hidalgo • Batán de Abajo • Bejía • Punta del Hidalgo — 130
- 23 Punta del Hidalgo • Chinamada • Las Carboneras — 133
- 24 Las Carboneras • Taborno • Roque de Taborno • Casa Carlos — 136
- 25 Casa Carlos • Afur • Playa de Tamadiste • Afur • Roque Negro • TF12 — 139
- 26 Pico del Inglés • Barranco de Tahodio • Santa Cruz — 143
- 27 Taganana • Afur • Taborno • Las Carboneras — 145
- 28 El Bailadero • Chinobre • Cabezo del Tejo • El Draguillo • Roque de las Bodegas — 149
- 29 Chamorga • Roque Bermejo • Faro de Anaga • Tafada • Chamorga — 152
- 30 Igueste • Barranco de Zapata • Playa de Antequera • Barranco de Antequera • Igueste — 155

Bus timetables — 159
Index — 164
Some bus and tram information — 168
Fold-out island map — *inside back cover*
Drawings of island flora — 24, 28, 129, 135

Preface

Tenerife has something for everyone — country lanes for strolling, nature trails for hiking, mountains to be scaled, and beaches where you can while away the day.

To absorb the island's beauty takes time. Her personality lies in the countryside. The bleak south is a mystery of dry terraced slopes, sliced through by deep ravines. The lush and green northern escarpment yields up forested hillsides rolling off the central massif, soon burgeoning with produce as it steps its way down to an indigo sea. Las Cañadas, the focal point of every visit, lies embedded in the island's backbone — a world apart, where strange hues and tormented rock forms are dominated by the majesty of El Teide.

In spring the island is a living tapestry of colour. This is the best time for exploring. The profusion of wild plants and flowers makes the island a botanical treasure. But no season is without its bloom and pot-pourri of colour.

Tenerife caters wonderfully for walkers, with well-marked trails criss-crossing an incredible kaleidoscope of landscapes: the Anaga — spectacular coastal scenery and laurel forests dripping with lichen and cushioned in moss; Las Cañadas — the unforgettable moonscape; Teno — a hidden world of tilting plateaus and deep chasms; the Orotava Valley — a lush chequerboard of fields and gardens embraced by pines.

But you needn't be a walker to appreciate Tenerife's beauty. The car tours, with their encompassing panoramas, will give you a taste of the landscapes. The picnic spots will, I hope, encourage you to meander just a little further off the beaten track. Then there are many short walks that require no great expenditure of energy and make a memorable day's outing.

My love for Tenerife first led me into the depths of the countryside in the early 1980s. My short strolls soon turned into longer rambles and these, in turn, became long hikes. I'd become an avid walker and explorer. The fact that I saw so few other walkers prompted me to write the first edition of this book — to encourage countryside enthusiasts to step off the usual touring routes, to see and feel the real Tenerife. Since then, of course, the island has become one of Europe's best-loved walking destinations. There's an unending source of weird and wonderful countryside just awaiting your exploration, and I hope that *Landscapes of Tenerife (Cañadas • Orotava • Teno • Anaga)* will help you find it.

Mass tourism, especially over the last few decades, has brought Tenerife both benefits and disadvantages. The people have seen their island undergo a great transformation. They are gradually losing great tracts of land to foreigners, who have no interest in being part of island life. This has dampened the natural Canarian warmth and friendliness, but it has not yet vanished altogether. A friendly smile of greeting will help, but I cannot recommend too strongly that you pick up at least a smattering of Spanish — this will make all the difference between having a good holiday and a truly memorable one.

— NOEL ROCHFORD

Publisher's note

We have left Noel's Preface unchanged, but in 2023/24 two things happened which might affect your walking holiday: a huge fire in 2023 and several anti-tourism protests in 2024. Thanks to the resiliance of the Canary pine (see page 44) and the efforts of the forestry workers, you would not suspect the damage done had you not seen the island before. However, some walks were still closed at press date. And although the protests were not against nature-loving walkers, *do your bit!* Take to heart the Country code and advice on pages 46-47 and read the updates mentioned inside the front cover.

Acknowledgements

I am very grateful to the following people:
For originally guiding me and advice: The Grupo Montañero de Tenerife
For her splendid drawings: my sister, Sharon
For ongoing updating: Conny Spelbrink, Jan Kostura and Pat Underwood who, between them, have rewalked all the routes for later editions.

Useful books

Be sure to pack a good standard guide to Tenerife to complement this *countryside guide*. And I highly recommend three 'classics', now out of print but available online from second-hand sellers: Bramwell, D and Z, *Wild Flowers of the Canary Islands,* London, Stanley Thornes; Cano, D M *Tenerife,* León, Editorial Everest; Cuscoy, L D and Larsen, P C *The Book of Tenerife,* Santa Cruz de Tenerife, Instituto de Estudios Canarios.

Also available from Sunflower (by Noel Rochford)
  Landscapes of Fuerteventura
  Landscapes of Gran Canaria
  Landscapes of La Palma and El Hierro
  Landscapes of Lanzarote
  Landscapes of Southern Tenerife and La Gomera
  Canary Island Walks

Getting about

There is no doubt that a **hired car** is the most convenient way of getting about Tenerife, and car rental on the island is extremely good value, especially if you shop around.

The second most flexible form of transport is a hired **taxi** and, especially if three or four people are sharing the cost, this becomes an attractive idea. If you're making an unmetered journey, do agree on the price *before* setting out: all taxi drivers should carry an official price list.

Coach tours are the most popular way of seeing many holiday islands; this is an easy way to get to know a place in comfort, before embarking on your own adventures.

My favourite way of getting about is by **local bus**. The system is very economical and reliable. The plans on the following two pages show you where to board buses in Puerto de la Cruz and Santa Cruz, as well as the Santa Cruz/La Laguna tram. On pages 159-163 you will find timetables for all the buses used for the walks and picnics in this book. But please do not rely *solely* on these timetables. Download bus timetables from the website below before you travel.

The local bus company is called TITSA. They operate a super-efficient website (**titsa.com**, with English version), which you can search for the latest timetables with route maps, journey planners, real-time bus arrivals. If you plan to make good use of the buses, be sure to get a daily (€10) or weekly (€50) pass. These are valid for all urban and inter-urban lines as well as the Santa Cruz–La Laguna tram. The bus stations are *very* well organised: see page 168.

It always pays to verify bus departures and returns for long journeys and less frequent services *before* setting out, and it always pays to arrive at your bus stop or station a bit *early!*

Heading west out of Puerto on a breezy day (Walk 1b)

PUERTO DE LA CRUZ

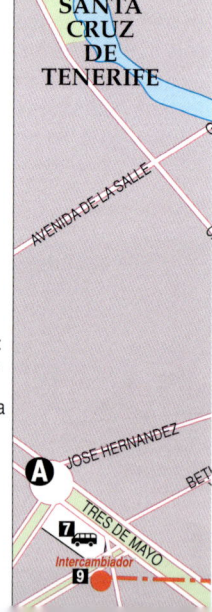

PUERTO DE LA CRUZ
1. Town hall (Ayuntamiento) and Tourist information
2. Castillo de San Felipe
3. Plaza Viera y Clavijo
4. Post office
5. Nuestra Señora de la Peña
6. Hotel Semiramis
7. Casino Taoro
8. Bull ring
9. Bus station
10. Hospital/24-hour first aid
11. Mirador de la Paz
12. Puerto Pesquero
13. Casa Iriarte
14. Mirador de la Costa

city exits

Exit A: to the TF320 to Icod and the TF5 westbound

Exits B and C: to the TF5 to La Laguna and Santa Cruz (the TF31 joins the TF312 at C)

🚐 A or C: stops for *outbound* Puerto buses used in this book

SANTA CRUZ
1. Plaza de España
2. Cabildo (local government headquarters), Tourist information, Archaeological museum
3. Post office
4. San Francisco church
5. Fine arts museum
6. Market
7. Bus station (Intercambiador)
8. Plaza General Weyler
9. Tram stop (see details on page 168)

city exits

Exit A (Avenida 3 de Mayo): to the motorways north (TF5) and south (TF1)

Exit B (Avenida Francisco la Roche): to San Andrés and the Anaga Peninsula

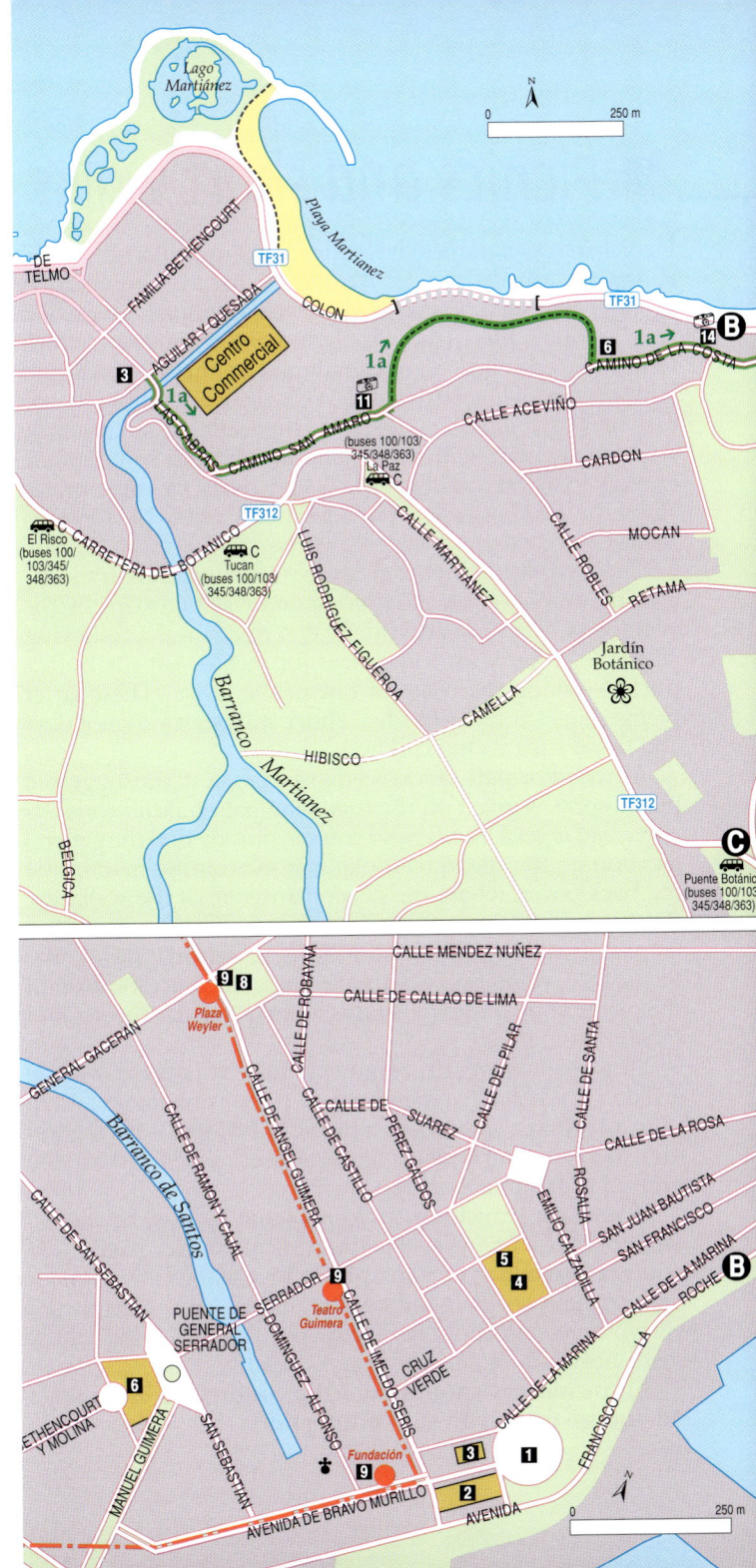

Picnics and short walks

Picnickers are extremely well catered for on Tenerife. Medio Ambiente (the island government's nature conservation agency) has set up several very well-equipped 'recreation areas' around the island. At these *zonas recreativas* (which tend to be crowded on weekends and holidays), you'll find tables and benches, barbecues, WCs, drinking fountains and play areas for children. They've also scattered simple little wooden shelters, with tables and benches, in some of the island's loveliest settings. You'll find many of these *chozas* along the TF21 (the 'Las Cañadas road') and in the Orotava Valley.

These **roadside picnic areas** are indicated both in the car touring notes and on the touring and walking maps by the symbol ⊼. They are also briefly described on the following pages, together with some ideas for picnics 'off the beaten track' — along the route of one of the walks. These latter picnic suggestions make **ideal short walks** for very hot days and those with young children.

All the information you need to get to any of the suggested picnic spots is given on the following pages. *Picnic numbers correspond to walk numbers*, so you can quickly find the general location on the island by looking at the touring map inside the back cover, where the general areas of all the walks are shown. I give transport details (🚐: bus numbers; 🚗: where to park), walking times, and views or setting. Beside the picnic title, you'll find a map reference: the exact location of the picnic spot is shown on this *walking map* by the symbol *P*, printed in green.

Please glance over the comments *before* you set off: if some walking is involved, remember to wear sensible shoes and to **take a sunhat** (○ indicates a picnic in **full sun**). It's a good idea to take along a plastic groundsheet as well, in case the ground is damp or prickly.

If you are travelling to your picnic by bus, be sure to arm yourself with up-to-date bus timetables (see page 7). **If you are travelling to your picnic by car**, be extra vigilant off the main roads: children and animals are often in the village streets. Without damaging plants, do park *well off* the road; **never** block a road or track.

All picnickers should read the country code on page 46 and go quietly in the countryside.

Picnic/short walk suggestions 11

3 CHOZA CHIMOCHE (map page 60, photo of similar setting page 61)

by car or taxi: 45min on foot
by bus: 45min on foot

🚗 at the Choza Bermeja or the Mirador de la Bermeja on the TF21, about 5km south of Aguamansa; see map on page 57). Car tour 1

🚐 348 to 'Choza Bermeja'.
Walk east on the forestry track just south of the Bermeja choza. You'll come to Choza Chimoche after a gentle climb of a little over 2km, with a height gain of about 75m/245ft, lasting about 45 minutes. A few minutes past here is another picnic spot, at the mouth of a dry barranco (the Barranco de los Llanos). Shade.

5 CHOZA EL TOPO (map page 65)

by car or taxi: 1h on foot
by bus: 1h on foot

🚗 La Caldera car park (TF21). Car tour 1

🚐 345 to La Caldera
Follow Short walk 5-1 (page 64) — an ascent of 100m/330ft. Views over Agua-mansa's valley. Shade.

Montaña de las Arenas, from the main road at La Crucita (Car tour 5, Walk 7, Picnic 7)

12   Landscapes of Tenerife (Cañadas • Orotava • Teno • Anaga)

6 LA CALDERA (map page 70, nearby photos page 71)

by car or taxi: up to 5min on foot
by bus: up to 5min on foot
🚗 La Caldera car park (TF21). Car tour 1
🚌 345 to La Caldera
Zona recreativa; *views over the Orotava Valley.*

7 LA CRUCITA (map pages 72-73, photos pages 11 and 58-59)

by car or taxi: 5-30min on foot
by bus: not easily accessible
🚗 off the side of the TF24 at La Crucita, 13km east of El Portillo (signposted). Car tour 5
Picnic by the side of the track, or explore either side of the TF24: to the west, you'll have views of the Orotava Valley and El Teide (photo pages 58-59); to the east you would overlook Montaña de las Arenas (photo page 11). Shade. **Note that both descents are steep and slippery.**

8 LAS CAÑADAS ROAD (touring map, photo page 57) 🏕

There are a few chozas on the TF21 (the 'Las Cañadas road'; Car tour 1) between Aguamansa and El Portillo — as well as the excellent Zona Recreativa Ramón Caminero (straddling the road, with tables, benches, barbecues, camping). All are signposted with the letter 'P' (parking), and all offer shade.

9 EL PORTILLO (map pages 82-83, photos pages 81) ○

by car or taxi: 5-20min on foot
by bus: 5-20min on foot
🚗 (TF21, Car tours 1, 5) or 🚌 348 to El Portillo
There are plenty of good picnic spots around El Portillo if you don't mind the lack of shade. During Walk 9 you would have similar views to those in the photos on page 81. No shade.

11 LOS ROQUES DE GARCIA (map page 88, photo pages 88-89) ○

by car or taxi: 15-30min on foot
by bus: 15-30min on foot
🚗 (TF21, Car tour 1) or 🚌 348 to the Parador de las Cañadas
Follow Walk 11 for a short time, or just amble about until you find a comfortable rock. Marvellous views of El Teide, Guajara and the weird rock formations, but the only shade is from the rocks themselves. Crowded.

12 PIEDRAS AMARILLAS (map page 93, photo page 80) ○

by car or taxi: 15-30min on foot
by bus: 15-30min on foot
🚗 (TF21, Car tour 1) or 🚌 348 to the Parador de las Cañadas
Follow Walk 12 (page 91) to the 'Yellow Stones'. Crowded. No shade.

13a CHANAJIGA (map page 94) 🏕

by car or taxi: up to 5min on foot
by bus: not easily accessible
🚗 Chanajiga: head south from La Orotava on the TF21, and after 9km turn right on the TF326 for Benijos/Palo Blanco. Some 1.6km past the centre of Benijos, turn left for Las Llanadas. Chanajiga is signposted off this road. Near Car tour 1
Zona recreativa *with full facilities.*

13b CAÑADA DE LOS GUANCHEROS (map page 94, nearby photo page 96) ○

by car or taxi: 15-55min on foot
by bus: 15-55min on foot
🚗 (TF21, Car tours 1, 5) or 🚌 348 to El Portillo
Follow Walk 13 (page 95) to picnic along the path not far above the Visitors' Centre (photograph page 96; 15min), or walk on to the cañada (55min). Limited shade (two cedars at Cruz de Fregel five minutes ahead).

Picnic/short walk suggestions 13

14 LA CORONA (map page 98, photo page 99) ○

by car or taxi: up to 5min on foot
by bus: 50min on foot

🚗 at the La Corona *mirador*. From Icod el Alto, continue west on the TF342 towards La Guancha. About five minutes west of Icod (2km), take the road left signposted for the La Corona *mirador*. Near Car tour 3
🚌 354 to Icod el Alto; then follow Walk 14 (page 80) — a very steep climb of 250m/800ft.
Overlooks the entire Orotava Valley to the eastern escarpment. Little shade.

15a EL LAGAR (map pages 102-103, photos page 101) 🌲

by car or taxi: up to 5min on foot
by bus: not easily accessible

🚗 at El Lagar: head west for La Guancha on the TF342. In the town, take the first turning left, just past the petrol station and keep straight uphill. From here on, the way to El Lagar is signposted. If approaching La Guancha from the west, take a right turn just *before* the petrol station. The last 5km to the picnic site is on stabilised but rain-rutted track.
Car tour 3
Large pine-shaded zona recreativa

15b LA RAMBLA (map pages 102-103, photo page 106)

by car or taxi: 10-15min on foot
by bus: 10-15min on foot

🚗 at the signposted Barranco de Ruiz picnic site on the TF5 some 2km east of San Juan de la Rambla
🚌 107, 108, 325 or 363 to the picnic site
The well-equipped Ruiz zona recreativa *is less than inspiring, but a good place to park and easily reached by bus. Follow the signposted lane opposite down to hamlet of La Rambla, and picnic on the stone seats by the Ermita de la Virgin del Rosario — on the coastal path followed in Walk 15b. Or stroll from there to Las Aguas or San Juan.*

16 LA MONTAÑETA OR LAS ARENAS NEGRAS (map pages 108-109, photos pages 16, 107) 🌲

by car or taxi: 5min-1h on foot
by bus: 5min-1h on foot

🚗 at La Montañeta. The TF336 climbs the slopes above Icod de los Vinos to join the TF82 above Erjos. La Montañeta lies halfway along this road. Park at the roadside chapel of San Francisco above La Montañeta. (The locals drive up the rough track all the way to Las Arenas Negras, but with a hired car you are not likely to be insured for tyre damage.) Car tour 3
🚌 363 to Icod de los Vinos, then
🚌 360 to La Montañeta
Picnic in the lovely setting by the chapel (ample shade and virtually no walking) or hike up to Las Arenas Negras: follow Walk 16 (page 109) — a steep climb of 250m/800ft. Shade of pines and full zona recreativa *facilities. Busy on weekends: to get away from the crowd, continue uphill past the picnic grounds for another 10-20 minutes.*

17 NEAR ERJOS (map page 114) ○

by car or taxi: 10-55min on foot
by bus: 10-55min on foot

🚗 at Erjos (on the TF82 between El Tanque and Santiago). Car tour 3
🚌 325 to Erjos
Follow Walk 17 (page 112) as far as you like. Soon there are views to El Teide, and you can picnic beside the track. Gentle climb back to your transport. Not recommended at weekends.

18a PUERTO DE ERJOS (map pages 116-117) ○

by car or taxi: 10-15min on foot
by bus: 10-20min on foot
🚗 in a lay-by on the south side of the pass: there are two lay-bys within 200m of the pass, on the TF82, 3km north of Santiago del Teide.
🚌 325 to Erjos: get off at Puerto de Erjos
Walk as far as you like up the narrow road that climbs to summit of Montaña Jala and choose an appealing spot (the landscapes on either side of the ridge are quite different). A 40 minute climb would take you to the summit — for a spectacular view over the northwest corner of the island. Limited shade at the roadside.

18b THE PONDS ABOVE ERJOS (map and photo pages 116-117) ○

by car or taxi: 10-20min on foot
by bus: 10-20min on foot
🚗 Restaurante Fleytas, 2km south of Erjos on TF82.
🚌 325 to Erjos: get off at Restaurante Fleytas, above Erjos
Follow Walk 18 (page 116) to the lush herbaceous basin with its pretty ponds, visible from roadside above. No shade.

19a LA TABAIBA PASS (map page 119, photo pages 32-33) ○

by car or taxi: 5-15min on foot
by bus: 5-15min on foot
🚗 at La Tabaiba, a pass signposted 'Mirador de Baracán', at km12 on the TF436 south of Las Portelas.
🚌 363, then 🚌 366 (see Walk 19, page 119)

Picnic 20b: bridge on the coastal path on the west side of Playa de las Arenas. From here the walkway heads further west, till it drops off into the sea at Punta del Fraile.

Follow the PR TF 51 trail from the mirador and parking area, to climb the ridge (Cumbres de Baracán) as far as you like. There are fine views of the El Palmar Valley and the ravine of El Carrizal. Limited shade.

19b LA SIETE (map page 119, photo pages 120-121) ○

by car or taxi: 10-20min on foot
by bus: not accessible
🚗 well off the end of the road in the hamlet of La Siete, 1km above Teno Alto (turn left up the *steep, narrow* road, past the bodega/village shop).
Walk along the track that continues off the road. In a few minutes you're looking into a deep valley. Head up to the right, to a natural hillside balcony and enjoy one of the best spots on the island, especially in spring, with views

Picnic/short walk suggestions

to El Teide and the hidden corners of Teno. Limited shade.

20a PUNTA DE TENO (map pages 122-123, photo page 124) ○

by car or taxi: up to 10min on foot
by bus: up to 10min on foot
🚗 at Punta de Teno, 8km from Buenavista (TF445), but see 'Important' at the top of page 29. Car tour 3
🚌 369 from Buenavista
Exquisite views of sea cliffs and the lava promontory at the lighthouse. The only shade is from the cliffs.

20b BUENAVISTA COAST (map pages 122-123 photos below and page 114) ○

by car or taxi: up to 20min on foot
by bus: up to 30min on foot
🚗 or 🚌 to Buenavista
Follow Short walk 20 (page 122) to the chapel at the start of the coastal path to Punta del Fraile — or walk/drive further west, perhaps as far as the bridge shown below. No immediate shade.

22 BATAN DE ABAJO (map on reverse of touring map) ○

by car or taxi: 10-15min on foot
by bus: 10-15min on foot
🚗 village car park, below Batán de Abajo. Turn off the TF12 0.8km west of Cruz del Carmen; keep right all the way to Batán.
🚌 274 to Batán de Abajo; the bus stop is at the village car park.
Walk uphill from the car park, then take the first left. Just past the village bar, turn right along an alley, signposted for Punta del Hidalgo. Walk to the second ridge, some 10

16 Landscapes of Tenerife (Cañadas • Orotava • Teno • Anaga)

minutes away. Superb views over this vast valley and its adjoining ridges, as well as the Barranco del Tomadero. No immediate shade.

23a PLAYA DE LOS TROCHES (map on reverse of touring map, photo pages 130-131) ○

by car or taxi: 10-15min on foot
by bus: 10-15min on foot
🚗 turning circle at the end of the TF13, beyond Punta del Hidalgo. Car tour 4
🚌 105 to Punta del Hidalgo
Follow Walk 22 (page 131) to this stony beach. Steep descent/ascent. The only shade is from the cliffs.

23b LAS ESCALERAS (map on reverse of touring map)

by car or taxi: 25-35min on foot
by bus: 25-35min on foot
🚗 Las Carboneras: turn off the TF12 1km east of Cruz del Carmen. Then keep left for Las Carboneras. Car tour 4
🚌 275 to Las Carboneras
Follow Alternative walk 23 (page 133) to Las Escaleras, overlooking two valleys. Easy climb/descent of 100m/330ft. Shade nearby.

23c MIRADOR DE AGUAIDE (map on reverse of touring map, nearby photo page 134) ○

by car or taxi: 15-20min on foot
by bus: not accessible
🚗 Chinamada: as for Picnic 23b above, then continue past Las Carboneras to Chinamada, where the TF145 ends.
From the plaza in Chinamada, walk behind the church and follow the signposted path (PR TF 10) to the mirador. Superb coastal views and outlook over Punta del Hidalgo. No shade.

24 NEAR TABORNO (map on reverse of touring map, nearby photos pages 136, 138, 146) ○

by car or taxi: 25-30min on foot
by bus: 25-30min on foot
🚗 Taborno: turn off the TF12 1km east of Cruz del Carmen. Then keep right for Taborno. Car tour 4
🚌 275 to Taborno

Detail from the lovely Ermita de San Francisco at La Montañeta

Follow Walk 24 from Taborno (page 137) to the top of the ridge reached in 30min. No shade.

25 AFUR (map on reverse of touring map, photos pages 141, 142) ○

by car or taxi: 15-20min on foot
by bus: 15-20min on foot
🚗 Afur: the turn-off is under 2km east of the turn-off to Pico del Inglés.
🚌 076 to Afur
Follow Walk 25 from Afur (page 140) to the big balancing rock. Quiet spot overlooking a winding barranco. The only shade is from the rock.

26 BARRANCO DE TAHODIO (map on reverse of touring map, photo page 144)

by car or taxi: 20-30min on foot
by bus: 20-40min on foot
🚗 Mirador Pico del Inglés. Car tours 2, 4
🚌 275, 076 or 077 to the Pico del Inglés turn-off, or 🚌 273 to the *mirador* itself
Follow Walk 26 (page 143) to the lookout point over the barranco and dam. There are also views to El Teide. Tiring climb to return. Shade.

28 PLAYA DE BENIJO (map on reverse of touring map, nearby photo page 28) ○

by car or taxi: up to 5min on foot
by bus: 10-15min on foot
🚗 near the beach, 4km past Taganana on the TF134. Car tour 2
🚌 946; ask to be put off at the Almáciga turn-off and walk east to the beach, a few minutes away.
Beautiful coastal views. The coast at nearby Almáciga is shown on page 28. No shade.

29 CHAMORGA OVERLOOK (map on reverse of touring map, photo page 153) ○

by car or taxi: 15-20min on foot
by bus: 15-20min on foot
🚗 Chamorga: the 71km-point in Car tour 2
🚌 947 from Santa Cruz to Chamorga at 10.15 *weekends only;* returns 16.30
The road ends just below a bar/shop. From here follow a path up behind and to the left of the bar and toilets, to the top of the ridge overlooking the village and its ravine. No shade. Steep, short climb of about 100m/330ft with a possibility of vertigo. Fine view back over the village and across the valley. Or picnic at the chapel setting shown on page 153.

30a IGUESTE (map on reverse of touring map) ○

by car or taxi: 5-10min on foot   by bus: 5-10min on foot
🚗 Igueste, at the end of the TF121. Car tour 2
🚌 945 to Igueste
Follow Walk 30 (page 156) but, where main walk bears left up Pasate Julio, descend to the right, to the stony beach — a pleasant spot with fine coastal views, but no shade. Photo of Igueste page 158.

30b LAS CASILLAS (map on reverse of touring map) ○

by car or taxi: 30-40min on foot
by bus: 30-40min on foot
🚗 some 10km east of El Bailadero, on a sharp bend in the TF123, by a lane to the Las Bodegas cemetery and a sign for the PR TF 5 to 'Iguesté'. Park at the side of the cemetery road. Car tour 2
🚌 947 (not Sundays; see notes for *Short walk 30-2* on page 155)
Follow Short walk 2 on page 155 to Las Casillas. Shade nearby.

Touring

Car hire on the island is extremely good value, especially if you book online before travelling. **Roads** vary from the wide divided motorways (always busy) to narrow and precipitous lanes (about which I warn you in advance). Two things to watch out for: **signposting** in built-up areas and at some roundabouts can be confusing, and some new **three-lane highways** (like the TF1 south of Santiago del Teide, not used for any tour) are potentially dangerous.

The car tours are numbered in order of importance: if you will only tour for a day or two, there is no question about priorities. Don't miss Tour 1! If you don't mind a long day's touring, you can combine Car tours 2 and 4.

The touring notes are brief: they include little history or information readily available in standard guides or in free leaflets obtainable from the tourist offices. The facilities and 'sights' of the towns are not described for this same reason. Instead, I concentrate on the 'logistics' of touring: times and distances, road conditions, and seeing some of 'hidden' Tenerife. Most of all, I emphasise possibilities for **walking** and **picnicking** (the symbol *P* alerts you to a picnic spot; see pages 10-17). While some of the references to picnics 'off the beaten track' may not be suitable during a long car tour, you may see a landscape that you would like to explore at leisure another day, when you have more time.

The fold-out island map can be opened opposite the touring notes and contains all the information you will need outside the towns. The tours have been written up with Puerto as departure/return point, but can easily be joined from other centres. Plans of Puerto de la Cruz and Santa Cruz, with city exits, are on pages 8 and 9. **Symbols** used in the text are explained in the map key; note that only *isolated* hotels and restaurants are highlighted: you will find them (as well as medical centres) in all major villages.

Allow ample time for stops: my times include only short breaks at viewpoints labelled 📷 in the notes. Calculate time for **detours** as well: villages, picnics and walks shown in ( ) at the top of the tours are only accessible via *detours*.

Distances quoted are *cumulative km from Puerto.* A key to the symbols in the touring notes is on the touring map.

Las Teresitas beach, from the TF121 not far east of Santa Cruz (Car tour 2)

Car tour 1: THE OROTAVA VALLEY AND LAS CAÑADAS

Puerto de la Cruz • La Orotava • Las Cañadas • Los Gigantes • Guía de Isora • Adeje • Playa de las Américas • Playa de los Cristianos • Vilaflor • Las Cañadas • Puerto de la Cruz

239km/148mi; 7-8h driving; Exit B from Puerto (plan pages 8-9)
En route: ⏸ at La Caldera, Las Cañadas road, Chio, Las Lajas; Picnics (see *P* symbol and pages 10-17): 3, 5, 6, 8, 9, 11, 12, (13a), 13b; Walks 1-13

This long excursion requires a very early start. Don't be put off by dark clouds over the north, because very often Las Cañadas and the south are soaking up the sunshine! All roads are in good condition, and signs of fire damage in the Orotava Valley are few.

This dramatic circuit begins gently, in the still-lush Orotava Valley, with few reminders of the 2023 fires. We wind our way up into the pines on the higher slopes and soon, in sunlight, the landscape changes abruptly: we cross the vast, bare plateau of the Cañadas crater. Fields of jagged scoria layer the floor with the occasional sprinkling of *retama,* a hardy broom. Southward, heading towards the coast, some calm returns to the landscape, as the smooth mounds of the more recent volcanoes emerge. Picturesque villages on the severe southern escarpments show us another face of Tenerife — a more sombre beauty.

Leave Puerto via Exit B (Avenida de Colón) or C (Carretera del Botánico), then follow the TF21 through **La Orotava★** (7km ⛽🅿⊕M). As La Orotava is so close to Puerto, save your visit for another day. The town is best seen during the festival of Corpus Christi (May/June): the streets are carpeted in flowers, and in the main square intriguingly beautiful religious 'paintings' are made from the multi-coloured sands of Las Cañadas. Visit Calle de San Francisco, with its magnificent old mansions, lovely courtyards and wooden balconies. Also of interest are the main church (La Concepción, 18C, the botanical gardens, and the church of San Juan, which commands a superb view of the Orotava Valley.

The road (🅿✕) rises past the turn-off to Benijos (15km 📷✕; *P*13a with ⏸ at Chanajiga). Old lichen-covered walls hide well-tilled plots, and scatterings of aged chestnut trees line the route to **Aguamansa★** and the **trout farm** (20km ⬅◉❀WC), where Walks 2-4 begin and Walk 6 ends. Just after, turn left uphill to **La Caldera★** (22km △✕⏸WC*P*5 and 6a). This tiny crater, where Walks 5-7 begin and Walk 8 ends, is a superb viewpoint over the green Orotava slopes and down to the sea. From here keep climbing, past the Mirador Piedra La Rosa★ (📷), a viewpoint to the famous rock shaped like a rose, and several roadside picnic areas (⏸; *P*3 and 8).

Walks 8, 9 and 13 begin at **El Portillo** (37km ⏸✕*P*8, 9, and 13b), where the **Cañadas Visitors' Information Centre** (*i*WC) welcomes you to 'another planet' — **Las Cañadas★**. The constant change in colour and rock formation within the encircling crater walls is

Left: driving through Las Cañadas, within the walls of the crater shown overleaf, leaves a never-to-be-forgotten impression (Car tour 1).

the highlight of this tour — and, I imagine, of your visit. Sharp streams of rock give way to smooth mounds of pumice and fine scoria, while sunken sea-beds of gravel create 'pools' along the floor. Majestic Teide is with you wherever you go, and Montaña de Guajara, rising out of the encircling wall like an abutment, rivals El Teide in beauty.

The leisurely drive through this wonderland (📷 at Minas de San José and Tabonal) takes you past the turn-off to Montaña Blanca and El Teide (Walk 10, photos on pages 85 and 87). A few kilometres beyond the cable car station (Short walk 9), you come to the **Parador de las Cañadas** (52km ▲✕*i*P12) and the **Roques de García**★ (📷*P*11), the troupe of rocky upthrusts shown on page 90, overlooking the vast Ucanca Plain. Walks 11 and 12 begin and end here. Barely a kilometre further on, you'll be intrigued by the patches of green and blue rock in the bank at the side of the road ('**Los Azulejos**') — even more striking when seen from the plain below. Mirador Llano de Ucanca (📷) affords yet another perspective over this setting.

At the pass of **Boca Tauce** (59km) fork right on the TF38 for 'Guía de Isora'. Pico Viejo is the prominent dark mound on the right. For several kilometres, the road cuts its way through the dark lava flows. Pines reappear, scattered across the landscape, and smooth volcanic cones remind you of the last volcanic outbursts. Set amidst this scenery is the lovely **Chio** *zona recreativa*

Car tour 1: The Orotava Valley and Las Cañadas 23

(⛺🍴). Past here, Las Estrellas restaurant (✕📷) is a good viewing point over the southwest coast.

At a junction (88km 🅿), leave the TF38 and continue to the right along the TF82 towards Santiago del Teide. At **Tamaimo** (93km 🅿), an attractive village sheltering below a high rocky protrusion, turn left on the TF454. Greenhouses for tomatoes now cover the landscape as the route winds down to Los Gigantes.

At the 98km-mark, at a junction, keep right for Puerto de Santiago. **Los Gigantes** (100km 📷) is a modern tourist complex, set against a backdrop of sheer cliffs★ rising vertically out of the sea. From Los Gigantes make for nearby **Puerto de Santiago** (🅿⊕) and the adjoining Playa de la Arena. Continue past **Alcalá** (🅿) to tranquil **San Juan** (110km 🅿).

From San Juan head up the TF463 towards **Guía de Isora** (🅿⊕), a small country town sitting on bare rock slopes. Passing below the town (120km), continue to the right on the TF82. Then turn off left to **Adeje**★, 2km off the main road (135km). Park on the main street. The town rests below crags, and a table-topped mountain, Roque del Conde, fills the background. A great chasm, the Barranco del Infierno★, runs past the edge of the village. (The ascent of Conde and hikes into and above the Barranco del Infierno are described in *Landscapes of La Gomera and Southern Tenerife*, as are several other walks between here and Vilaflor.) Adeje is also well known for its *pollo en mojo* (chicken with spicy sauce), which makes it a good spot to stop for lunch.

Leaving, follow the main street back to the TF82, which takes you to the motorway towards Santa Cruz (🅿). Now you have a choice of fine sandy beaches, easily accessible from the motorway. The best known are at the lively resorts of Costa Adeje/Fañabé, Playa de las Américas and Playa de los Cristianos. But the main tour bypasses these built-up areas, to head inland again via Arona. Take

Las Cañadas from the summit of El Teide (Walk 10), with Gran Canaria rising in the distance above a sea of clouds. The following figures will give you some idea of the immensity of Las Cañadas: its diameter is almost 16km/ 10mi and its perimeter an astounding 45km/28mi. Much of it is surrounded by craggy, inconsistently-peaked walls, the highest point being Montaña de Guajara (Walk 12), 500m/1650ft above the crater floor, but all of 2717m/ 8905ft above sea level. El Teide is the majestic centrepiece.

Aeonium manriqueorum

Lavandula pinnata

Rock rose (Cistus)

Margarita del Teide

Exit 72 (the same motorway exit as for Los Cristianos). Joining the old TF28 (⊕ and camel park) follow it for 4.5km to a junction, then head left on the TF51 (passing the Jungle Park). **Arona** (150km 🍴🚌📷) has a charming shady church square, surrounded by balconied old houses. The village enjoys a fine outlook down over the coast, marred only by the dull plastic sheeting covering the 'glass'houses.

Vineyards on walled slopes surround the TF51 to **Vilaflor** (164km 🍴🚌⊕📷 **M**), the highest town on the island at 1161m/3810ft. Nestled on the edge of a plain, this mountain settlement looks up onto the steep, forested inclines that run down off the high mountain spurs above.

From Vilaflor follow the TF21 back to Las Cañadas, driving through some of the loveliest Canary pine forests on the island. Pino Gordo, a *mirador* 2km past Vilaflor, sits amidst these regal ancient pines (📷). The road takes you through some spectacular rugged mountain landscapes (🍴 at 175km, Las Lajas *zona recreativa*).

You re-enter the crater at Boca Tauce (181km). The twisted uprising of rock here is more impressive when approached from the south. Bear right along the TF21 and return to Puerto under the late afternoon or evening sun. The mood of Las Cañadas changes under this soft light. Shadows fall across the crater floor, colours mellow, and low clouds begin curling over the crater walls, as you retrace your outgoing route to **Puerto** (239km).

Car tour 2: THE RUGGED ANAGA PENINSULA

Puerto de la Cruz • Cruz del Carmen • Pico del Inglés • Roque Negro • El Bailadero • Chamorga • Taganana • Almáciga • Benijo • San Andrés • Igueste • Puerto de la Cruz

171km/106mi; 5-6h driving; Exit B from Puerto (plan pages 8-9)
*En route: ⊓ at El Bailadero; Picnics (see **P** symbol and pages 10-17): (25), 26-30; Walks 24-30*
Driving is slow in this mountainous terrain, with fairly heavy tourist traffic.

Fill up with petrol before starting out; there are no petrol stations in the Anaga, and none on the touring route until San Andrés. **Hint:** *Beyond Las Mercedes, refer to the large-scale map of the Anaga on the reverse of the touring map.*

T his excursion takes us amidst the mountains of the Anaga Peninsula. Twisting along the backbone of this range, the road is one continuous *mirador*. Inland, lost in these rugged contours, lie tiny remote villages, clinging to rocky nodules and buried in *barrancos*. And along the coast, quiet and secluded little bays unravel.

Laurels, heath trees and pijaras *in the Pijaral*

Take the motorway (TF5, 🚗) towards Santa Cruz. To avoid starting the day in a nightmare of traffic, keep on the motorway *past* La Laguna, then take Exit 8A for the Anaga (TF13). Follow sign-posting for Tegueste at first. Just past Las Canteras, at the round-about, go right for the Anaga, joining the TF12 and immersing yourselves in the coolness of the laurel forest (🌲). Stop at **Cruz del Carmen★** (📷🅿🍴ℹ), the information centre for the Anaga walking trails, to pick up the latest trail information; new trails are always being opened and there may be some not shown on our Anaga map inside the back cover.

A kilometre further on, turn right for **Pico del Inglés** (40km 📷*P*26), another fabulous *mirador*, where Walk 26 begins. Then head back to the main road (TF12) and turn right. Restaurante Casa Carlos, 1km further on, is the landmark where Walk 25 starts and Walk 24 ends. Solitary houses speckle the ridges segmenting the isolated Afur Valley. Some 3km along, turn left to **Roque Negro** (TF136), a small village over-shadowed by an enormous black basalt rock (48km 📷). The village square serves as a good look-out point: Afur can be seen far below in the shadows of these high crests (photo on page 141) and a wild beach, the Playa de Tamadiste, lies beyond the village. I highly recommend a 4km detour to Afur (*P*25), just to experience the friendly bar and to stretch your legs with a walk to the picnic spot. The main tour returns from Roque Negro to the TF12 and heads left, after 3km

Car tour 2: The rugged Anaga Peninsula 27

passing a forestry house (56km ⌂☞) where Short walk 27-2 begins.

At the 59km-mark, fork left for **El Bailadero**★ (☞), where Walk 28 begins. Just 0.5km past the hideous green buildings at this settlement (they are apparently private and date from before this area was put under protection), you pass the charming Albergue de Anaga (♦), blending perfectly into the landscape — a truly get-away-from-it-all place to stay. From here on the road is flanked by dense laurel forest, and you soon pass a sign, '**El Pijaral**'. Then, 0.8km past the 4km road marker, you'll no doubt spot some parked cars: this is a good place to start Walk 28, if friends will play chauffeur — and you have a permit!

Just before the 6km road marker, from the **Mirador de las Chamucadas** (☞), you'll have good views down over Igueste, a seaside village built across the mouth of a *barranco* (visited later in the tour). Then, 250m further on, a sign for El Pijaral on the left alerts you to a track used in Alternative walk 28-2: even without a permit, you could stop here to admire the laurels, heath trees and *pijaras* (see pages 24-25). The starting point for Short walk 30 lies about 3km further on, when you reach a road off right to the Las Bodegas cemetery. You could stretch your legs here by descending to the deserted hamlet of Las Casillas (*P*30), with another fine view down to Igueste.

Descending in S-bends into open rocky terrain, pass a turn-off to Las Bodegas itself (69km), sheltered in a narrow *barranco*, half a kilometre downhill. La Cumbrilla is the village perched high on the ridge under which the road passes. **Chamorga** (*P*29), the most isolated village on Tenerife, lies at the end of the road, a couple of kilometres further on. A loose smattering of white dwellings, the hamlet snuggles into the sides of a *barranco*, shaded by palms and loquat trees. Walk 29, only accessible by car, begins and ends here. (If you're an experienced hiker, then try *Alternative* walk 29 — a must!)

From Chamorga return to the Taganana turn-off (left, just below El Bailadero). Some 2km further down, turn left again (⌂). After passing through a tunnel under the Bailadero *mirador*, you overlook a landscape of razor-sharp ridges

Walk 27 rises from Taganana, the village shown above, to Taborno and then Las Carboneras.

Almáciga, perched above the coast (Car tour 2, Walk 28)

cutting down to the sea. **Taganana** (91km ♣⊕*P*27), where Walk 27 begins and Short walk 25-2 ends, is a brilliant array of white houses spread across the tumbling lower crests of the valley. Palms and colourful gardens make this settlement extremely photogenic. Roque de las Animas (the Ghosts' Rock) towers straight above the road 1km beyond the village. **Roque de las Bodegas** (93km), with its roadside restaurant, is a busy tourist stop. Past **Almáciga, Benijo** (96km *P*28b) is just a few cottages and a beach. Restaurante El Frontón, with good food and magnificent views, is a pleasant place to take a break. From here the track followed in Short walk 28 continues to isolated El Draguillo (which also boasts a dragon tree, but not as impressive as the one shown opposite!).

Retracing your route through the tunnel, follow the TF12 down the Barranco de San Andrés to the south coast. Notice, between KM5 and KM3, the plant life on the cliffs at the right — a textbook lesson in Canarian flora. At **San Andrés** (115km 🚍), turn left on the TF121 for Igueste, quickly coming to the fine viewpoint over Las Teresitas shown on page 18. The palms here, on Tenerife's only golden-sand beach, add a touch of the tropics. Picturesque **Igueste** (123km ✕*P*30; Walk 30) sits at the end of this cliff-hugging coastal road.

From Igueste follow the coast all the way to Santa Cruz, then pick up the motorway (🚍) back to **Puerto** (174km).

cardón
(Euphorbia canariensis)

Car tour 3: SPECTACULAR NORTHWEST SETTINGS

Puerto de la Cruz • San Juan de la Rambla • Icod de los Vinos • Garachico • Punta de Teno • Teno Alto • Santiago del Teide • Icod el Alto • Puerto de la Cruz

Important: The road to Punta de Teno is closed to traffic (see overleaf). It will take at least two hours to go to the lighthouse and back by bus, so you may wish to save Punta de Teno for another day. If so, turn left for El Palmar on the TF436 at its junction with the TF445.
153km/95mi; 6-7h driving; Exit A from Puerto (plan pages 8-9)

En route: ⊼ Barranco de Ruiz, Los Silos, Buenavista, road to Teno Alto, Santiago del Teide, around La Guancha, near the Mirador de Garachico; Picnics (see *P* symbol and pages 10-17): (15, 16), 17-20; Walks 14-21
Except for the TF5, roads are narrow and winding. Some will find the Teno Alto and Masca roads vertiginous.

A backdrop embroidered in greens highlights the small and picturesque villages, precipitous sunken valleys, superb coastal settings and sheer shadowy peaks that characterise the landscapes visited on this circuit.

The famous dragon tree at Icod de los Vinos

30 Landscapes of Tenerife (Cañadas • Orotava • Teno • Anaga)

Head west from Puerto on the TF5 motorway. When it ends, continue ahead (still the TF5). This coastal road passes below cliffs towering up to the left; breakers crash below on the right (10km 🕼 **Mirador de San Pedro**, Walk 1b; 13km 🅿 **Barranco de Ruiz**).

San Juan de la Rambla (16km 🍴) is a charming fresh-white village overlooking the sea. Las Aguas, a neighbouring village on the rocky shoreline below, is a picture-postcard scene glimpsed just before San Juan. All the way from Puerto to the northwestern tip of the island, you're immersed in banana palms and bright seasonal blooms. These settings really come alive when you explore them on foot during Walk 15b.

Continue along the TF5, then take the TF42 into **Icod de los Vinos★** (26km ⛪🍴⊕), on the fertile vine-growing slopes below El Teide. The 16th/17th-century San Marcos Church merits a visit. Just below the lovely church square is Icod's famous ancient dragon tree … and the 'Butterfly House', a newer tourist attraction. Nearby Playa de San Marcos, a resort that never took off, is a small sandy beach surrounded by dark jagged cliffs (a 5km return detour).

Leave Icod on the TF42, hugging the coast and passing manorial homes amidst banana plantations. Then you come into **Garachico★** (32km ⛪🚌🍴⊕M). This beautifully-situated village, once an important port, was destroyed by a volcanic eruption in the early 18th century. But a few buildings of interest survive: the 16th-century San Miguel Castle, the Baroque palace of the Marqués de Adeje, the 17th-century Convent of San Francisco, and the Church of Santa Ana (founded in 1548). Garachico is otherwise known for its inviting natural rock pools. The Roque de Garachico, rising up off the shore, bears a cross to protect the little town from another catastrophe.

Continuing west on the TF42, you skirt **Los Silos** (38km ⛪🍴🅿) on a bypass road just south of the church square shown on pages 110-111, passing banana plantations behind surprisingly attractive cinderblock walls. Walks 16 and 21 would take you into the impressive deep ravines that open out onto this village. Further along this fertile coastal plain lies **Buenavista** (42km 🍴⊕🅿*P*20b), where Walk 20 ends. The village is walled in by high sharp crags, and gorges and valleys cut back into this cataclysm of rocks.

Just past the Plaza de San Sebastián, where there is a small chapel on the right, turn off left for 'Punta de Teno' on the TF445 … only to be stopped about 3km along at a barrier. To protect the fragile ecosystem (and because of rockfall) you can no longer drive to the point. But Titsa buses leave *from the barrier* every hour, costing only 1€. Sit on the right going to the point and on the left returning! About 2km from the barrier there are especially fine views from **Punta del Fraile** (🕼), where the island falls away into an indigo sea (as does the path for Short walk 20!). The road continues to wind its way around and under rough indented cliffs, high above the sea, and then descends to the lighthouse on the dark volcanic promontory of **Punta de Teno** (52km 🕼*P*20a). This protected peninsula is one of the richest botanical areas in the Canaries.

Return to Buenavista (61km): at the junction, turn right on the

View to Garachico from the Monument to the Canarian Emigrant

TF436 for El Palmar. El Palmar's lush curving valley lies well hidden above the coastal plain. A steep climb through rocky terrain covered in prickly pear, *vinagrera, verode, tabaiba* and wild geraniums leads you up past magnificently-terraced slopes. Walk 17 ends at **El Palmar** (67km). Just outside the village you pass to the right of 'Cake Hill': the Montañeta de Palmar, shown overleaf and on pages 122-123, was so neatly quarried for building materials that it resembles a sliced cake.

Opposite, look on the right for a narrow country lane signposted to Teno Alto and follow it. (This turn-off is the starting point for Walk 20.) A steep climb (69km 🅿) takes you up to **Teno Alto** (75km ✕🖻) — a tiny outpost of farms scattered across a tableland eaten away by enormous valleys. Scrub and pastures share the slopes. Alternative walks 18-1 and 18-2, as well as Walks 19 and 20 pass through Teno Alto. Lunchtime? Try the simple home cooking in the bar/restaurant here, especially the *cabrito* (kid) and *garbanzos* (chickpeas) … and don't miss the wine. But if you're picnicking, and it's not too windy, then try the picnic spot a kilometre uphill (***P***19b): take the *steep, very narrow* road that climbs to the right of the village shop/bodega. The road ends at another hamlet, La Siete. Use notes on page 14 to reach one of the best spots on the island (photo on pages 120-121 and map on page 119).

Return to the El Palmar road and head right. At the KM12 road marker you come to the pass of **La Tabaiba**; park here for the **Mirador de Baracán** (89km 🖻***P***19a) — to take in the dramatic difference between the El Palmar and Masca valleys — the former broad, smooth and sweeping, the latter sharp and turbulent. Walk 19 begins here, and Alternative walks 18-1 and 18-2 cross here en route to Teno Alto.

Winding down into deep gorges on an increasingly vertiginous road, several lay-bys and *miradors* allow you to pull over to appreciate the magnificent scenery, with especially fine views over **Masca★** (94km 🖻), a favourite village among the islanders themselves. (Masca is a very popular walking base, and its *barranco* is explored in *Landscapes of Southern Tenerife and La Gomera*.) The valley — perhaps best seen with mist swirling around the heights — is green, green, *green*, with a wealth of Canarian flora on display.

Climbing out of the gorges, you cross a pass with spectacular views of El Teide; behind you, La Gomera, La Palma, and — if you're lucky — El Hierro can be seen on the horizon. **Santiago del Teide** (100km ✝🅿⊕🅿) rests in a shallow valley just below. Meeting the main road in the village (TF82), turn left past the pretty

Car tour 3: Spectacular northwest settings

church on the right and the eucalyptus-shaded picnic area on the left, to head north towards Icod de los Vinos. A great change takes place as you leave Santiago's treeless valley and enter the herbaceous greenery that envelops **Erjos** (*P*17), where Walk 17 begins. The pass of **Puerto de Erjos** (103km 📷*P*18a, 18b) separates the two basins. One kilometre below the pass sits friendly Restaurante Fleytas — with great home cooking and pastries; it's the perfect afternoon tea stop. Walk 18 begins at the restaurant, and Short walk 18 ends here.

The unkempt countryside soon gives way to cultivated plots of vegetables and fruit trees. The Camel Centre is passed just above **El Tanque** (112km 🍴), a long strung-out village. A turn-off left in the village would take you to the Mirador del Lomo Molino (1km west; 📷✕), with expansive views all along the northern slopes as far as Tacoronte. At the roundabout on the far side of the village, be sure to take the third exit (the first is a 'no entry'), to keep to the TF82, *not* the newer TF5 highway. A couple of kilometres below El Tanque lies the **Mirador de Garachico** (📷✕ and nearby 🅿), from where you have the best outlook over the village setting and its offshore rock.

Superb views accompany the descent through hillside villages to Icod. Approaching the town, head right for 'La Guancha' at the roundabout and drive through **Icod**. Just 3km further on, at another roundabout, turn right on the TF342 (also signposted to La Guancha). The road climbs through rocky farmland to **La Guancha** (125km 🍴⊕ and nearby 🅿; *P*15), where Walk 15a ends. From here head straight along the TF342 to another farming area set on steep slopes, **Icod el Alto** (136km 📷🍴), where Walks 14 and 15a begin. The Mirador La Corona is 3km up a side road to the right as you enter, but the Mirador El Lance (📷✕; Walk 15b), built into the escarpment just past the village, is more convenient and offers the same far-reaching views. (Besides ... La Corona's shrine can't compete with El Lance's well-hung Guanche statue.)

Rounding the escarpment and leaving the village, the road, cut into the sheer rock face, affords tremendous views on the descent into the Orotava Valley.

Coming into **Los Realejos** (🍴⊕ and oldest ✝ on Tenerife), *carefully* follow the complicated one-way system through the town. Just beyond Los Realejos Bajo, pick up the motorway heading east; then leave at Exit 36 to head back east into **Puerto** (153km).

From the Mirador de Baracán you can take in the dramatic difference between the sharp, narrow Masca (top) and smooth, broad El Palmar (left) valleys.

Car tour 4: QUIET CORNERS OF THE ANAGA

Puerto de la Cruz • Tacoronte • Bajamar • Punta del Hidalgo • Batán • Las Carboneras • Taborno • Pico del Inglés • La Laguna • Puerto de la Cruz

140km/87mi; 6h driving; Exit B from Puerto (plan pages 8-9)
En route: Picnics (see *P* symbol and pages 10-17): 22, 23a-b, (23c), 24, 26; Walks 22-27
This can be an afternoon's drive, but it's better to spend a leisurely day: driving will be slow on the narrow winding roads. **Hint:** *beyond Punta del Hidalgo, refer to the large-scale map of the Anaga on the reverse of the touring map.*

Drive down to the coast and take a dip in the sea-water pools (there are several choices), continue up to the summits of the Anaga and wend your way down into silent *barrancos* with dramatically-sited villages. Go for a stroll in the laurel forest, then perhaps finish the day on a cultural note: saunter around the streets of La Laguna.

Take the motorway (TF5) from Puerto as far as Exit 21 for El Sauzal. Pass under the motorway, then go right immediately on the TF152 for **Tacoronte** (18km ✝🅿⊕). The wooden statue of Christ in the 17th-century church here is attributed with numerous miracles and is revered by many of the islanders. Immediately past the plaza, turn left on the TF16 and follow it all the way to **Tejina** (28km 🅿), where a one-way traffic system operates. At an unsigned T-junction, go left. At the large roundabout outside Tejina, follow signs for Bajamar. Colourfully blooming bushes and creepers, together with large banana plantations, enliven the landscape along here. The village's tidal pools make the small-scale resort of **Bajamar★** (32km 🅿⊕) a popular swimming spot. A backdrop of severe rocky ridges and ravines overshadows the settlement, and an abundance of xerophytic plants clings to the dark, abrupt inclines.

Continue on the same road to **Punta del Hidalgo★** (35km △📷🅿*P*23a). It lies along a slight bay with a rocky beach, across from Bajamar. The road ends past the village, at a turning circle where high craggy crests fall into the sea in the setting shown on pages 130-131. Walks 22 and 23 set out from here.

Return to the roundabout outside Tejina and follow 'La Laguna'. The same signposting leads you through **Tegueste** (46km 🅿). **Las Canteras** (51km 🅿) straddles a crest. At the roundabout in the village, take the second exit, turning sharp left onto the TF12 and heading up into the

34

magnificent laurel forest. The **Mirador de Jardina** (⌘) on the right, 4km from Las Canteras, affords captivating views of the lush green undulating hills outside La Laguna. Under 2km (⌐) further on, fork left for 'Batanes', to make for the isolated village of Batán, hidden in a valley deep in the spine of the peninsula. Keep right all the way downhill. Some 8km of winding road (TF143) brings you to **Batán** (*P*22), superbly sited in stunning mountain scenery. Having come all this way, why not walk to the picnic spot described on pages 15-16; you'll be amazed at the sheer hillside terraces and the paths that reach them.

Back on the TF12, keep left for **Cruz del Carmen**★ (74km ✕♣ ⌘*i*), with a Visitors' Centre of particular interest to walkers. Beyond this viewpoint you leave the dense forest for a brief time, as you drive down to two more

View west from the Mirador de Jardina to El Teide (right) and the Anaga from Casa Carlos (Walks 24 and 25)

beautifully-situated villages — Las Carboneras and Taborno: 1km past the turn-off to Pico del Inglés, go left. At a fork, keep left (TF145) for Las Carboneras (downhill to the right lies Casa Carlos, where Walk 24 ends and Walk 25 begins). Valleys open up as you descend, and Punta del Hidalgo reveals itself for a moment. Roque de Taborno, shown on page 146, is a prominent landmark sitting high atop the opposite ridge. At a further fork, again keep left. **Las Carboneras**★ (85km *P*23b) sits glued to a hill, encircled by cultivation. Walks 23 and 27 end here; Walk 24 starts here. Chinamada (Walk 23, *P*23c), the tiny village of cave dwellings shown on page 134, is a further 2.5km along, should you wish to visit it.

Now return to the fork passed earlier (TF138) and turn left. After descending a forested ridge, you come into **Taborno**★ (90km *P*24), where small dwellings are dispersed along the crest of the ridge, rising high above two deep *barrancos*. Walks 24 and 27 both pass through the hamlet.

Go back to the main road and turn right. Then head left to **Pico del Inglés** (99km *P*26). Perched on the spine of this range that divides the island north and south, the *mirador* offers views down into the hidden Afur Valley, captures snippets of the coast, and looks out towards the island's guardian, El Teide. Walk 26 descends from here to Santa Cruz. From Pico del Inglés make for the university town of **La Laguna**, then return to **Puerto** (140km).

Car tour 5: THE SUN-BAKED SOUTH
Puerto de la Cruz • La Laguna • La Esperanza • El Portillo • Güímar • Arico • Candelaria • Puerto de la Cruz

224km/140mi; 6h driving; Exit B from Puerto (plan pages 8-9)
En route: ⌂ at Las Raices, Fuente Fría, Monte Los Frailes; Picnics (see *P* symbol and pages 10-17): 7, 9, 13b; Walks 7, 8, 9, 13

Part of the TF24 (between La Esperanza and the Arafo turn-off) is often enshrouded in low-lying mists. No petrol stations en route between La Esperanza and Arafo (68km).

From the greenest to the driest, from the highest to the lowest, and from forested to naked — this drive takes it all in. The inclines along the southern flanks of the island, missed by most tourists, are a dramatic contrast to the rich green slopes of the north.

Leave Puerto by Exit B or C and zip along the motorway (🍴) to La Laguna, where this tour *really* starts. About 28km along, turn off for La Esperanza and El Teide (TF24). Lush green pasturelands lie along the way to **La Esperanza** (34km 🍴), as you ascend the spine of the island, the Carretera Dorsal. This whole area was devastated by fire in the summer of 2023, but the forestry workers have done a splendid job of clearing. Beyond La Esperanza, keep right at the two junctions you encounter. Before long, the regenerating pines will forest the crest in deep shade. In the meantime, you have a number of *miradors* to enjoy. The *zona recreativa* Las Raices is passed on the left (39km ⌂) just before you reach the first *mirador*, **Montaña Grande** (40km 📷), looking all the way down to Santa Cruz and up to the Anaga range. But my favourite part of the tour, deep in the Corona Forestal (the island's crown of trees) used to lie around the KM16 road marker, where unfortunately the **Forestal Park★** adventure centre (⌂) was closed because of the fires when last seen. Next comes the **Mirador Ortuño** (📷), with views to the pine-robed slopes of El Teide. You pass the Arafo turn-off soon after: you'll be returning to this road later in the tour. A detour to the right leads to the *miradors* of **Chimague** and **Chipeque** (📷): the latter, much loved by the local

The charming town of La Laguna

Guímar and its pyramids (right); below: at Candelaria statues of ten former Guanche chiefs guard the seafront.

people, also looks out over the northern slopes from Teno to the Anaga. The pines here are regenerating nicely.

La Crucita (60km 📷*P*7; photos pages 11 and 58-59) is the point where pilgrims cross the TF24 on their way from the north to Candelaria. Walk 7 follows this ancient route. As you near the pass at the top of the road, the pines subside and rocky protrusions, covered in *retama,* take over the landscape. Later the terrain changes again, as rich volcanic tones — maroons, purples, russets, wines, greys and blacks — flow in and out of each other. A couple of kilometres further on, a section of the roadside bank attracts your attention with its grey and white horizontal stripes. You pass the turn-off for the Observatorio de Izaña (69km; iac.es; English pages).

El Portillo (75km ✗🅰*i*WC *P*9, 13b) is the starting point for Walks 8, 9 and 13. Turn round here and head back along the TF24 for 20km, to the Arafo turn-off passed earlier in the tour. You now descend to the southern slopes. Fire-damaged pines accompany you partway on this descent but, as you approach the lower slopes (🅰 at Monte Los Frailes), loose scatterings of chestnuts take over. The Güímar basin opens up ahead, revealing corners with great ravines cutting back deep into the steep escarpment. High brown stone terraces step the slopes of this productive agricultural centre. Vineyards, interplanted with vegetables, cover the greater part of the land. Bypass the centre of Arafo (where Walk 7 ends) and watch for a brown sign, 'Pirámides Güímar',

indicating your right turn if you want to visit the famous pyramids (**M**)★. Otherwise, go straight on through **Güímar** (116km 🅿⊕). Keep to the left of the church, then turn right along the *avenida*. At the T-junction turn right, to rejoin the TF28 for Fasnia.

This road winds in and out of shallow ravines before climbing out of the basin along the eastern escarpment, from where you have a superb view over the valley and towards the Anaga. From here on, the monotone landscape becomes more harsh. Trees have vanished, save for the fine-branched Jerusalem thorn bordering the

roadside. In April and November, its yellow blossoms cheer up this countryside. You'll notice, too, masses of roadside caves — squared, arched, and with doors or gates. Often the doorways open into enormous chambers.

Fasnia (133km 🚏⊕) is a pleasant country village set back off the road. Between here and Arico there are few settlements, and the land looks almost abandoned. The restaurant just uphill from the petrol station at **Arico** (147km 🚏⊕) makes a good lunch stop. Turn left here on the TF625, down to the motorway (TF1 🚏), then head left for Santa Cruz. After 24km turn off to **Candelaria**★ (179km ✝🚏⊕). The basilica (1958) houses the 'new' statue of Nuestra Señora de la Candelaria, the island's patron saint. (The original statue was supposedly found in 1390 by Guanche herdsmen and was lost in a tidal wave in 1826.) The large square on the seafront near the modern church is quite impressive, with red-rock statues of Tenerife's ten former Guanche chiefs.

Some 12km from Candelaria, be sure to take the TF2 'Autopista del Norte' connection, to bypass Santa Cruz and join the TF5 back to **Puerto** (224km).

Walking

This book covers most of the best walking on Tenerife — enough ground to keep even the most energetic hiker going for over a month. Since this guide is based on Puerto, I've included all the best walks in the Orotava Valley and Las Cañadas, but don't miss the Teno and Anaga peninsulas!

I hope you will also make up your own walk combinations. I've shown where my routes link up on the walking maps, and the fold-out touring map shows the general location of all the walks. But only join up walks by using routes described in this guide or the officially waymarked trails. 'Official' trails, very well signposted, are highlighted in yellow on our walking maps: thus even if the trail is not described in detail in my notes, you can still use them with confidence to short-cut (or 'long-cut') any of my walks.

There are walks in this book for everyone.

Beginners: Start on the walks graded 'easy', and be sure to look at all the short and alternative walks — some are easy versions of the long hikes. **You need look no further than the picnic and short walk suggestions** on pages 11 to 17 to find a large selection of fairly easy rambles.

Experienced walkers: If you are used to rough terrain and have a head for heights, you should be able to tackle all the walks in the book, *except those colour-coded black* (see opposite). Of course, you must take into account the season and weather conditions: in rainy weather some of the *barranco* walks will be unsuitable; in strong winds or snow do not plan excursions to the mountains! And always remember that **storm damage, fires or bulldozing can make these routes unsafe at any time!** *Do* follow the route as described in this book. If you have not reached one of the landmarks after a reasonable time, go back to the last 'sure' point and start again.

Experts: Provided that you are used to sheer, unprotected drops and scree, *and provided that conditions are still as described in the notes,* you should be able to enjoy all my walks.

All walkers: *Do* check the update service described on the inside front cover of the book before you travel!

Grading, waymarking, maps, GPS

There is a quick overview of each walk's **grade** in the Contents. But almost all the walks have shorter and/or alternative versions. In the Contents we've only had space to show the *lowest grade of a main walk:* for full details of grading, see the introductory remarks about the walk itself. Here is a brief overview of the three gradings:

● easy-moderate — ascents/descents of no more than about 300-500m/1000-1800ft (easy on the lungs, perhaps less so on the knees); good surfaces underfoot; easily followed

● moderate-strenuous — ascents/descents may be over 500m/1800ft; variable surfaces underfoot — you must be sure-footed and agile; possible route-finding problems in poor visibility

● expert — only suitable for very experienced hillwalkers with a head for heights; hazards may include landslides or balancing on the narrow ledges with no respite from constant exposure

Any of the above grades may, if applicable, be followed by:

❗ *danger* of vertigo — you must have a very good head for heights

Waymarking and **signposting** have been brought up to 'Euro' standards on most routes. There are three types of waymarking:

Walkers' signposts at La Caldera: at the top is a standard GR sign; its wine-red livery is repeated on the sign below, where the GR131 coincides with the yellow/white PR trail to Mamio. You'll also see green/white stripes for SL walks and orange stripes for mountain bikers. This photo was taken in 2024, when the TF 35 was closed: the authorities have tried to put tape over landmarks and times, but walkers peel it off.

■ *Red and white* waymarks indicating GR routes ('Grandes Recorridos': long-distance footpaths);
■ *Yellow and white* waymarks indicating PR routes ('Pequeños Recorridos': short trails of up to six hours);
■ *Green and white* waymarks indicating SL routes ('Senderos Locales': local trails, up to about 10km long).
■ For all these routes, two parallel stripes (=) mean 'continue this way'; right-angled stripes (⌐) indicate a 'change of direction'; an '✗' means 'wrong way'.

Trail maps should be available at the visitors' centres at El Portillo (for the Cañadas) and Cruz del Carmen (for the Anaga), but log on to **tenerifeon.es/en**, the official site of the island government (the 'Cabildo'), for an excellent **interactive trail map**, which can be enlarged and downloaded as an app. It shows alerts due to fire risk and **trail closures**. I have printed the trail numbers existing at time of publication on the walking maps and highlighted in yellow any official trails not described in the notes. But new trails are being cut all the time (and existing trails sometimes closed!), so you may find some not on our maps. On the website mentioned above you can learn about the island's many protected natural areas, fire levels during your visit, dates of mouflon control affecting walks, and much more.

The **maps** in this book are based on Openstreetmap mapping (see page 2), but have been very heavily annotated from notes and GPS work in the field. It is a pity that we have to reproduce them at only 1:50,000 to keep the book to a manageable size; quite a few walkers buy both the paperback *and* our downloadable pdf files so that they can print the maps at a larger size — or you can enlarge them on a colour photocopier.

Free **GPS tracks** are available for all my walks: see the Tenerife page on the Sunflower website. Please bear in mind, however, that GPS readings should *never* be relied upon as your sole reference point. Conditions can change at any time — especially on Tenerife, where mountainsides come down overnight. And those of you who cannot be bothered to use GPS on the ground could nevertheless enjoy opening the GPX files in Google Earth to preview the walks in advance!

Where to stay

For walkers **Puerto de la Cruz** is the best base. Attractive Puerto has a *very* efficient bus service and a wide choice of accommodation. Most of the walks described are easily accessible from here; the remainder require a few bus changes (making for long days, but little inconvenience). However, recognising that **the south** has become the island's major tourist centre, the bus timetables include some important connections from the Playas. (*Walks* in the south are described in *Landscapes of Southern Tenerife and La Gomera*.)

Consider spending a night or two at the uniquely sited, incredibly romantic **Parador de las Cañadas** (paradores-spain.com), gazing at the stars … and arriving at the Teide cable car before the queues form! If you're adventurous, you could also stay at the Refugio de Altavista on El Teide: see page 84. Finally, if you're not tied into 'package' accommodation, there are hotels in La Laguna and Santa Cruz, closer to the Anaga walks — as well as a hostel near El Bailadero, right in the heart of the Anaga (the Albergue Montes de Anaga; see alberguestenerife.net). For the Teno, try the hotels in Garachico and San Marcos, near Icod de los Vinos.

Weather

Island weather is often unpredictable, but there are a few signs and weather patterns that may help you forecast a walking day.

Tenerife is blessed with year-round walking weather. The north, unfortunately, has more than its fair share of rain, but pleasant temperatures. The south soaks up the sun. Wind strikes the southern coastline, but rain is a rarity.

Weather patterns are influenced by two **winds**:

Walk 25: fifteen minutes up the Barranco del Agua you look straight onto a sheer rock face clinging to the ridge. Two steps out the front door and these cave dwellers would tumble into the gorge…

The majestic Canary pine plays a very important ecological role in water retention (as described in the third paragraph on page 66). This is the reason for the continuous planting of trees in denuded areas of the forest: to feed the underground reservoirs, the *galerías*. From these *galerías* (tunnels), water is piped to all parts of the island. Tenerife relies very heavily on these water sources, because there are no natural wells and few streams with a permanent flow of water.

Below is a *galería* at Las Hayas, near El Lagar. The 'railway tracks' are often seen near *galerías*, where a great deal of soil has been excavated — one of the water tunnels in Walk 16 is 3.5km long!

But the tree also proved its worth after the wildfires in 2023. The Canary pine *(Pinus canariensis)* is among the earth's most fire-resistant: it drops its lower branches as it ages, so that fires can not climb up its trunk. Not only that, but Canary pines are one of the few pine species that can resprout needles from buds beneath their barks (epicormically). You will see this, for instance, on Car tour 5: where the pines look like childrens' drawings of stick figures, slender, but 'lumpy'. The tree at the left was sprouting epicormically in 2024.

the northeasterly trade winds (the *alisio*) and the easterly or southeasterly wind from the Sahara (the *calima*). Two other winds blow very infrequently: a northwesterly wind from the north Atlantic and a southwesterly wind from the tropics. Both carry heavy rains and storms. In winter this usually means snow in the mountains. Only the 'westerlies' carry clouds that blanket Las Cañadas. Luckily these winds are very rare.

The northeasterly trade wind, the *alisio,* which prevails for much of the year, is easily identified by low-lying fluffy clouds — which add so much character to your photos. These clouds hover over the north for much of the year. They sit between 600-1500m/2000-5000ft. Above these heights, clear blue skies prevail, the Cañadas being the only beneficiaries!*

The *calima,* quite different, brings heat and dust. The temperature rises considerably, and the atmosphere is filled with very fine dust particles. This weather is more frequent in winter than in summer. It seldom lasts more than three or four days. These days are always good for walking (but in summer stay under tree cover!); even if it's a little warm, the sky is cloudless, although a bit hazy.

The only wind that could really spoil your day is the one from the tropics. It *always* brings heavy rains which cover the whole island. This wind is recognisable from its uniform cloud cover. Fortunately it rarely blows.

The winds bring fresh breezes off the sea, making the days very pleasant for walking. And remember, the clouds don't block out the sun altogether; especially on the heights, you will tan (or burn) due to the combination of sun and wind. Don't forget a sunhat! On the other hand, when walking at the higher altitudes, one must always be prepared for the *worst* as well: all seasons can be experienced in one day!

Nuisances

Dogs, in general, aren't a problem. However, if you do a lot of walking on the island, you are bound to meet at least one unfriendly monster, rightly guarding his territory. You may wish to invest in a 'Dog Dazer', an ultrasonic device which frightens dogs off without harming them. These are available from various sources on the web.

---

*In winter the Orotava walks are at their best very early, between 08.00-11.00. After that clouds and mist usually hide all the views. It is often chilly and rainy, too, even when it's sunny at Puerto. So in winter head for the Cañadas and coastal areas of the Anaga. And even if you are based around Puerto, pack a copy of *Landscapes of Southern Tenerife and La Gomera:* If the weather is bad in the north, several excellent walks in that book are within easy reach of Puerto, especially if you have a car.

Hunters may startle you with bursts of gunfire, but they present no other worries. They come out in force on weekends and holidays — always trailed by yapping dogs. The hunting season is from August through December.

Give chained **billy goats** a wide berth; they don't like intruders! Other than that, you've no other pests to worry you on Tenerife — there are no poisonous snakes or insects.

What to take

Please don't attempt the more difficult walks in this book without the proper gear. For each walk, the *minimum year-round equipment* is listed. Where walking boots are required, there is no substitute: you will need to rely on the grip and ankle support they provide, as well as their waterproof qualities. All other walks should be done with stout lace-up shoes with thick rubber soles, to grip on wet, slippery surfaces.

You may find the following packing list useful:

walking boots, spare bootlaces
mobile/smartphone/gps
waterproof rain gear (outside summer months)
long-sleeved shirt (sun protection)
first-aid kit, including bandages
walking pole(s)
windproof (zip opening)
trail map(s) (see page 41)
extra pair of socks
sunhat, sunglasses, suncream
up-to-date bus timetable
small rucksack
bottle with water-purifying tablets
long trousers, tight at the ankles
insect repellent
knives and openers
lightweight fleece, warm fleece
swimming things
groundsheet
torch, whistle, compass

Please bear in mind that I've not done *every* walk in this book under *all* weather conditions. Use good judgement to modify my lists according to the season.

Country code

A code for behaviour is very important on Tenerife, where the rugged terrain can lead to dangerous mistakes.

- **Only light fires** at picnic areas with fireplaces.
- **Do not frighten animals.** The goats and sheep you may encounter on your walks are not tame. By making loud noises or trying to touch or photograph them, you may cause them to run in fear and be hurt.
- **Walk quietly** through all hamlets and villages, and take care not to provoke the dogs.
- **Protect all wild and cultivated plants.** Don't try to pick wild flowers or uproot saplings. Leave them for other walkers to enjoy. Obviously fruit and other crops are someone's private property and should not be touched.

- **Leave all gates just as you found them**, whether they are at farms or on the mountainside. Although you may not see any animals, the gates have a purpose: they are used to keep goats or sheep in (or out of) an area. Animals could be endangered by careless behaviour.
- **Never walk over cultivated land.**
- **Take your litter away with you** — or, if answering 'calls of nature', *bury it*.

Advice for walkers

The following points cannot be stressed too often:
- **At any time a walk may become unsafe** due to storm damage or bulldozing. If the route is not as described in this book, and your way ahead is not secure, do not attempt to go on.
- **Walks graded for experts** (with the ● black circle) may be unsuitable for winter, and all mountain walks may be hazardous then.
- **Never walk alone** and *always* tell a responsible person *exactly* where you are going and what time you plan to return. Remember, if you become lost or injure yourself, it may be a long time before you are found. Four is the best walking group: if someone is injured, two can go for help, and there will be no need for panic in an emergency.
- **Do not overestimate your energies** — your speed will be determined by the slowest walker in your group.
- **Transport connections** at the end of a walk may be vital.
- **Proper shoes or boots** are a necessity.
- **Mists** can suddenly appear on the higher elevations.
- **Warm clothing** is needed in the mountains; even in summer take some along, in case you are delayed.
- **Extra rations** must be taken on long walks.
  Mobile or smartphone, compass, whistle, torch, first-aid kit weigh little, but might save your life.
- **Always take a sunhat with you**, and in summer a cover-up for your arms and legs as well.
- **A stout stick/walking pole** is a help on rough terrain and to discourage the rare unfriendly dog.
- *Do not take risks!* Some of the walks cross remote country and can be both **very cold and potentially hazardous.** Distances on Tenerife can be deceptive — perhaps with exhausting descents into and ascents out of hidden *barrancos* between you and your goal. Only link up walks by following routes indicated on the walking maps; don't attempt to cross unmapped terrain.

Spanish for walkers

In the tourist centres most people speak English. But once out in the countryside, a few words of Spanish will be helpful, especially if you lose your way. Here's a way to communicate in Spanish that is (almost) foolproof. First, memorise the few short key questions and their possible answers below. Then, when you have your 'mini-speech' memorised, always ask the many questions you can concoct from it **in such a way that you get a 'sí' (yes) or 'no' answer**. Never ask an open-ended question like 'Where is the main road?' Instead, ask the question and then *suggest the most likely answer yourself.* For instance: 'Good day, sir. Please — where is the path to Erjos? *Is it straight ahead?*' Now, unless you get a '*sí*' response, try: '*Is it to the left?*' If you go through the list of answers to your own question, you should eventually get a '*sí*' response — probably with a vigorous nod of the head — and this is more reassuring than relying solely on sign language.

Following are the two most likely situations in which you may have to practice some Spanish. The dots (...) show where you will fill in the name of your destination. Approximate pronunciation of place names is in the Index.

■ Asking the way
The key questions

English	Spanish	pronounced as
Good day,	Buenos días	**Boo**-eh-nos **dee**-ahs
sir (madam, miss).	señor (señora, señorita).	sen-**yor** (sen-**yor**-ah sen-yor-**ee**-tah).
Please —	Por favor —	**Poor** fah-**voor** —
where is	dónde está	**dohn**-day es-**tah**
the road to ... ?	la carretera a ...?	la cah-reh-**teh**-rah ah ...?
the footpath to ...?	la senda de ...?	lah **sen**-dah day ...?
the way to ...?	el camino a ...?	el cah-**mee**-noh ah ...?
the bus stop?	la parada?	lah par-**rah**-dah?
Many thanks.	Muchas gracias.	**Moo**-chas **gra**-thee-as.

Possible answers

English	Spanish	pronounced as
is it here?	está aquí?	es-**tah** ah-**kee**?
straight ahead?	todo recto?	**toh**-doh **rec**-toh?
behind?	detrás?	day-**tras**?
to the right?	a la derecha?	ah lah day-**reh**-chah?
to the left?	a la izquierda?	ah lah eeth-kee-**er**-dah?
above/below?	arriba/abajo?	ah-**ree**-bah/ah-**bah**-hoh?

■ Asking a taxi driver to return for you

English	Spanish	pronounced as
Please	Por favor	**Poor** fah-**voor**
take us to ...	llévanos a ...	**Yay**-vah-nos ah ...

| and return | y volver | ee vol-**vair** |
| for us at … | para nosotros a … | **pah**-rah nos-**oh**-tros ah … |

Point out the time when you wish him to return on your watch.

An inexpensive phrase book or searching the web will help you compose other 'key' phrases and answers.

Organisation of the walks

The 30 main walks in this book are grouped in four general areas: the Orotava Valley, Las Cañadas, the northwest (including the Teno Peninsula), and the Anaga Peninsula. I hope that the book is set out so that you can plan your walks easily — depending on how far you want to go, your abilities and equipment, and the season. You might begin by looking at the fold-out island map inside the back cover. Here you can see at a glance the overall terrain, the road network, and the location of all the walks. Quickly flipping through the book, you'll see that there is at least one photo for every walk.

Having selected one or two potential excursions, turn to the relevant walk. At the top of the page you'll find planning information: distance/time, grade, equipment, and transport details. If the grade and equipment specifications are beyond your scope, don't worry: *there's almost always a short or alternative version of a walk,* and in many cases these are far less demanding of agility and equipment.

When you are on your walk, you will find that the text begins with an introduction to the overall landscape and then quickly turns to a detailed description of the route itself. The **large-scale maps** (see notes on page 42) have been annotated to show key landmarks. **Times** are given for reaching certain points in the walk, based on an average walking rate of 4km/h, with extra time allowed for ascents and steep descents. *Do compare your own times with those in the book on a short walk, before you set off on a long hike.* Remember that I've included only *short stops* at viewpoints; allow ample time for photography, picnicking and swimming.

The following **symbols** are used on the walking maps:

══════	motorway	❷ P	waypoint; picnic (pages 10-17)
══════	main road/secondary road	A ⊼	*choza;* picnic tables
──────	minor road or lane	♪ ∩	*galería,* tap, spring/cave
──────	jeep or motorable track	⌇ ∆	pylon, wires/rock formation
------	path or steps	🚗 🚌	car parking/bus stop
3→ 3→	main walk/alternative walk	❗	danger! danger of vertigo!
PR TF 7	'official' waymarked trail	⸸ † ⊞	church/shrine/cemetery
2→	other described route	■ 📷	specific building/best views
──────	watercourse *(canal)*	— 824 —	height (metres)

Walk 1: TWO COASTAL WALKS FROM PUERTO DE LA CRUZ

Walk 1a: Puerto de la Cruz • Playa del Bollullo • Café Vista Paraíso

See also town plan pages 8-9
Distance: 8km/5mi; 3h10min
Grade: ●❗ fairly easy along the coastal stretch with ups and downs on steps, but the climb to the café and bus stop (just under 350m/1150ft) is strenuous and somewhat vertiginous, with loose stones and rubble underfoot initially.
Equipment: stout walking shoes (boots preferable), light fleece, sunhat, suncream, rain-/wind-proof, picnic, water
Transport: The walk starts in Puerto de la Cruz (bus stop El Risco or La Paz). Return on 🚌 101 from the TF217 at Cuesta de la Villa (not in the timetables, but runs every 20 minutes to La Orotava, from where there are many buses to Puerto)

Alternative walk
1 **Puerto de la Cruz — Playa del Bollullo — Puerto de la Cruz:** up to 11.5km/7.1mi; 3h45min; ● easy-moderate; access and equipment as main walk. *This version avoids the steep climb to Café Vista Paraíso.* Follow the main walk to Playa del Ancón, then retrace your steps to ❹, the El Rincón bus stop. Either take 🚌 376 (daily; hourly in summer, approximately every 2 hours in winter) back to Puerto or else retrace your steps via the **Barranco de la Arena** along your outgoing route.

Walk 1a: Coastal walk east of Puerto de la Cruz 51

Right on your doorstep, Walk a is an excellent 'starter', with magnificent seascapes of towering cliffs. And if vertigo is a problem, or the climb to Café Vista Paraíso looks too daunting, opt for the Alternative walk. Then, another day, if the weather on the coast holds fine, head west as well — from César Manrique's lovely Playa Jardín, follow Walk b along the coast to the palm groves and banana plantations of Rambla de Castro.

Referring to the town plan on pages 8-9, **start out** at the palm-graced **Plaza Viera y Clavijo** (○), at the top end of Avenida Aguilar y Quesada. Follow Calzada Martiánez over the bridge to the shopping centre, and almost immediately turn left up steps on Camino las Cabras. You rise up to Calle San Amaro, where you again turn left. This pretty promenade is also stepped. Not far uphill, veer left to the **Mirador de la Paz** (**1**), from where you have a superb view over Puerto.

From here descend to the **Camino de la Costa**, a walkway built into the face of the cliffs, with a striking outlook all along the coast. After five minutes, it takes you up to a street (Leopoldo Cólogan Zulueta) just beside the Hotel Semiramis (**30min**). Turn left and, when the street swings right, keep straight on, now on a tarmac lane (still the Camino de la Costa). Passing below the last apartment block on the right, and a CAR PARK, the way takes you under the main Carretera del Este, and a neatly-paved lane comes underfoot. You look up at verdant slopes sliding off into the sea and disappear amidst banana plantations.

Some ten minutes from the underpass a stepped path (missing its handrail when last seen) takes you down into the little **Barranco de la Arena**, filled with strong-scented lavender, *tabaiba*, marguerites, and sticky-leafed *lengua de gato*. Out of the ravine you meet a small road (**2**; **55min**), where a right turn leads up to El Rincón; keep left. (*The Alternative walk can return to this point and retrace steps.*) At the next junction, turn left again. Soon you're heading along the cliff-top above **Bollullo Beach** — a particularly pretty spot.

Just past the Bollullo Restaurant (**3**; open daily; **1h**),

View down over Playa del Bollullo

leave the lane and turn off on a path that heads along the cliff-tops, scattering lizards galore. Minutes along, you pass the path down to Bollullo Beach at **Punta del Fraile**. Remember, if you go down to the beach, where there is a café, swim only on calm days! The main walk returns from this point.

(As an alternative, it is possible to head right on a path at the right-hand side of the wall — the original path above the coast, at the left of the wall, has fallen away. Soon this path swings inland, and you ascend an overgrown *barranco*. A flight of steps then takes you up a precipitous escarpment to the narrow El Rincón road — it's a vertiginous stretch, but shortens the walk.)

For the main walk, retrace your steps to the Bolullo Restaurant and then climb the road to the bus stop at **El Rincón** (**4**; **1h40min**) and the San Diego Restaurant (closed Sun/Mon). Keep following this narrow road and, at a junction a couple of minutes along, where a road to the right is signed to La Orotava, keep left. (You may see a handwritten sign here: 'Digital Nomads — Mass Tourism OUT of our Beaches'. The lane ends at a GATE (**5**; **1h55min**), beyond which a private track runs to **Finca El Ancon** (**6**), set in splendid isolation on a high promontory with spectacular sea views, in the midst of their 100 acres of vines and fruit. To the right is your ascent route to Café Vista Paraíso. But first turn *left*, squeezing to the left of the gate and following signposting down a sealed path and then steps to **Playa del Ancón** (**2h10min**), where you'll doubtless be joined by surfers and swimmers. The cliffs around here make a lovely picnic spot.

Returning to the ascent point for Café Vista Paraíso takes about 15 minutes. Now head steeply and *carefully* uphill; initially the walled-in path is quite skiddy, with loose stones underfoot. The zigzags afford fine views of the lower Orotava Valley. Some 35 minutes uphill, steps bring you up onto a road, where you turn left. Here live the *crème de la crème* — all behind high walls. **Café Vista Paraíso** (**7**; **3h**) lies a couple of minutes along (closed Mondays). Enjoy the delicious cakes and pastries, as well as the spectacular views to Puerto and the Orotava Valley!

Then climb the steps to the right just past the café and turn left on the road at the top. Turn right over the TF5 and, at the junction that follows, head right uphill, to **Cuesta de la Villa**. The BUS STOP (**8**; **3h10min**) is just over to the right, where you meet the TF217.

Walk 1b: From Puerto de la Cruz to the Mirador de San Pedro
See also town plan pages 8-9 and photo on pages 6-7
Distance: 6km/3.7mi; 2h

Grade: ● fairly easy, with ascents of 200m/650ft and descents of about 100m/330ft
Equipment: stout walking shoes (boots preferable), light fleece,

Walk 1b: Coastal walk west of Puerto de la Cruz

sunhat, suncream, rain-/windproof, picnic, water
Transport: The walk starts in Puerto de la Cruz (Loro Parque bus stop). Return on 🚌 107, 108, 325 or 363 from the Mirador de San Pedro on the TF5.
Alternative walk: Puerto de la Cruz — Mirador de San Pedro — Barranco Ruiz — San Juan de la Rambla: 12.5km/7.8mi; 4h; ● surprisingly ambitious, with ups and downs of about 600m/1970ft overall. Equipment as main walk, but *boots mandatory*. Access as main walk; return on 🚌 107, 108, 325 or 363 from San Juan de la Rambla. Only recommended for brave souls: there is *no path* between Playa del Socorro and La Rambla; you'll be stumbling over rocks for 2km — or, when the sea is high *and potentially dangerous* — retreating to the main road. *I have not done this walk myself and don't recommend it.* From **Playa del Socorro** (Nirvana for surfers, but I don't advise swimming here…) stumble over the rocks for 30 minutes, to pass below some ruined houses at **El Terrero**. After another 20 minutes or so you'll descend into the **Barranco de Ruiz** and climb out to a house on the far side. From here there's a lovely coastal path which you follow through **La Rambla** (1h10min from Playa del Socorro) and on to **Las Aguas**, with its bars and restaurants. Then take the access road up to **San Juan de la Rambla**. Use notes and map for Walk 15b on page 105.

This walk makes a fine pairing with Walk 1a. It's called the 'Sendero del Agua' — the 'Water Trail', because it passes through the Gordejuela area, with old water channels, springs and a ruined pumping station. Later the path runs through dense greenery at Rambla de Castro, where an old fort and mansion hide among the palms.

Referring to the town plan on pages 8-9, **start out** at the **Castillo de San Felipe** (O): follow the coastal promenade via the late César Manrique's colourful **Playa Jardín** for 1km, emerging near the entrance to Loro Parque (**15min**). Then carry on along the main road towards the white 'skyscraper' Precise Resort ahead. Just past the hotel, turn right on a cul-de-sac road past the blue Residencia Maritim, to the end of the street, with another high-rise hotel, the gold-balconied Acapulco III. The coastal path used to begin here, running to the right along the cliffs above **Playa de los Roques**. But now you come to a Y-fork after just a few metres, with a 'danger of rockfall' sign. You *can* still take the old coastal path — at your own risk. (If you do take it, after 500m turn right to a viewpoint towards the three offshore rocks for which the beach is named.)

There's an info board at this fork with a map of the new route, so take the wide cobbled path up to the left. After a few minutes it heads right and merges with Calle El Cedro. Keep to this road all the way to the **Mirador de los Roques** (❶; **45min**) in the **Romántica II** housing estate (which hardly merits its name…). Walk straight ahead along the road, initially past houses 26 and 24 on the left. Your road kinks left, then right (past some shops on the left). After rising, the road bends 90° to the left; the signposted coastal path continues on the right after 100m (initially as a lane).

The trail, now running quite high above the sea and edging terraces, passes below another development, **La Romántica I** (❷), then crosses an attractive bridge over the **Barranco El Patronato**. Now entering a large protected area called **Rambla de Castro**, you pass a stepped trail down right to **Casa Hamilton** (❸), the ruined four-story Victorian **Gordejuela** PUMPING STATION, built by an Englishman called Hamilton to power a flour mill and pump water from the Gordejuela springs to the Orotava vineyards and, later, banana plantations. It was abandoned when electricity replaced steam as a source of power.

Instead head left up the wide concrete track. After 500m the trail turns sharply right and narrows, soon dropping steeply into the **Barranco del Agua** (❹), which is also crossed on a bridge. Just after, at a fork, keep straight

Coastal outlook on the west side of San Juan de la Rambla, near the Alternative walk — a nice picnic spot

ahead on the main trail (the trail to the right goes down to stony **Playa de la Fajana** and another waterworks). In another 100m the trail forks again: left leads more directly to the TF5, but we keep right and pass above the **Forte San Fernando** (**5**). Our main route rises gently to **La Casona** (**6**) — the old manor house of the Castro family, for whom the 'Rambla' is named, and then climbs the wide trail to the TF5 and the **Mirador de San Pedro** (**7**; **2h**). There's a busy bar/restaurant here; your BUS STOP (with a KIOSK) is just to the left.

For those (fool)hardy enough to try continuing all the way to San Juan, take the trail below the bar/restaurant, past a chapel on the left. Joining a road after 450m, turn left and, at the T-junction almost at once, turn right down to **Playa del Socorro**. Please turn back if the surf's high — there are few escape routes!

Walk 2: AGUAMANSA TO CHASNA

Distance: 7.5km/4.6mi; 2h
Grade: ● contouring, then a fairly steep descent of 300m/1000ft
Equipment: stout shoes, sunhat, fleece, rain-/windproof, picnic, water
Transport: 🚌 345 from Puerto to Aguamansa (Timetable 2); journey time 45min; alight at the 'El Velo' bus stop. 🚗: park below the Restaurante Aguamansa, near the bus stop (28° 21.798'N, 16° 29.940'W)). Return on 🚌 345 (Timetable 2) from the TF21 — to Puerto (journey time 40min), or back to your car at Aguamansa. Alternatively, take 🚌 347 (Timetable 10) from Chasna to La Orotava
Alternative walk: Aguamansa — Chanajiga — Palo Blanco: 12.5km/7.8mi; 4h15min; ● moderate, with a climb of 100m/330ft and descent of 600m/1950ft; access and equipment as above. Return as Walk 14, page 97. Follow the main walk past the point where it turns down right at ❺ (at 1h06min). Continue along this track all the way to **Chanajiga**, referring to the map on page 98 once beyond Lomo Alto. Ignore the many turn-offs. LANDMARKS, CAIRNS OR OLD METAL PLATES along the way (sometimes almost illegible) include **Lomo de los Tomillos** (ⓐ; 1h40min); **Salto Bangarro** (ⓑ; 1h53min); **Lomo Alto** (2h15min); **Choza Cruz de Luis** (ⓒ; 2h40min). On reaching the tarred road, continue past it to the car park and **Chanajiga picnic area** (3h; map on page 98). To continue to **Palo Blanco**, an hour away, pick up Walk 14 at ❻ (the 2h45min-point, page 99).

This walk is a good starter — it should whet your appetite. The combination of greenery, flowering heather, and the bucolic charm of the highest farmland in the Orotava Valley makes this a pleasant afternoon's stroll.

Start out at the 'EL VELO' BUS STOP at **Aguamansa** (Ⓞ). Walk uphill towards Aguamansa, and then turn right uphill on the first lane (with a BARRIER prohibiting motorised traffic, but usually open, and just before the Restaurante Aguamansa on the other side of the road). You'll be ascending past the fenced TROUT FARM. If the gates aren't locked, you can get into the trout farm via the back entrance, four minutes up the lane. It's open from 10am to 3pm, and you can also see injured and rescued birds of prey there. Some 100m/yds beyond this entrance, just before a gate, climb the path to the left (sign: CALDERA). In three minutes you come to a SIGNPOSTED JUNCTION (❶) where the long-distance GR131 goes straight on to La Caldera or down right towards Teide. Keep straight on; you have joined the **SL TF 81**, signed for 'LOMO CHILLERO'. The main road is up to your left, and a track is below on the right briefly.

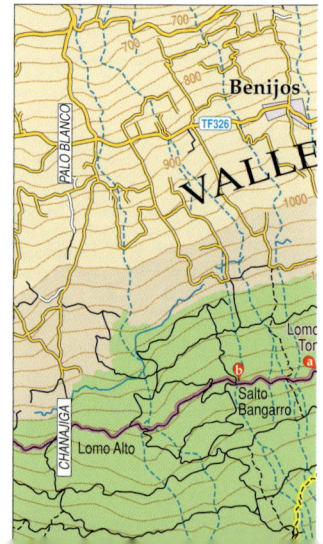

The famous Mirador Piedra La Rosa is on the TF21 not far above Aguamansa.

Coming up to the **Pista de Benijos**, the GR goes straight on to La Caldera through an underpass below the main road; keep right here for *'LOMO CHILLERO 0.9KM'* (❷). You pass a short-cut for the SL route (SL TF 81.1); then, at **Lomo Chillero**, the main SL TF 81 turns down right to the GR131 and loops back to Aguamansa. Keep ahead. The volcanic cone of El Teide may be in full view, peeping over the western wall of the Orotava Valley. But from this vantage point it's difficult to believe that this is Spain's highest mountain at 3718m/12,195ft!

View to El Teide and over the mist-shrouded Orotava Valley from La Crucita (Walk 7)

Some 50m or so further on, take a track off right to **Galería La Fortuita** (**3**; **30min**), one of the island's many water sources — as explained on page 44.

Back on the main track, ignore the fork off right within the next 20 minutes. A little over 10 minutes later, you enter a narrow gully and cross an overgrown stone bridge above a dry river bed with huge boulders. Within two minutes you pass **Galería Pino Soler** (**4**; **1h**); the two-storey GREEN BUILDING now houses the old railway engines.

Continue past the building, passing a first track on the right, for about 800m (about half a mile) to a second track on the right (**5**; 1h10min), and turn right downhill. *(But if you are doing the Alternative walk, keep straight on.)* This is the GR131 and also the Camino de Chasna, well waymarked with both red/white and yellow/white stripes. Follow these waymarks now till you reach a *zona recreativa*, **Cruz del Dornajito** (**6**; 1h35min).

When you access the lane leading away from this picnic area, the GR goes off to the right, but you continue all the way down the lane, to the main TF21 road in **Chasna** (**7**; **2h**). There's a stop for the 345 bus just to the left on the near side of the road; a stop for Puerto is diagonally opposite. But I suggest you walk downhill, round the hairpin bend, and catch your bus at the 'Camino de Chasna' bus stop outside the bar-café.

Walk 3: AGUAMANSA • LA CALDERA • CHOZA CHIMOCHE • LOMO DE LOS BREZOS • AGUAMANSA

See also photos on pages 67 and 71
Distance: 7km/4.3mi; 2h30min
Grade: ● easy-moderate climb/descent of 400m/1300ft; the descent from Lomo de los Brezos is steep and slippery.
Equipment: stout shoes, sunhat, fleece, rain-/windproof, picnic, water
Transport: 🚌 345 from Puerto (Timetable 2; journey time 45min) or 🚗 to/from the Aguamansa bus stop (at the entrance to the trout farm; 28° 21.653'N, 16° 29.782'W)
Short walk: Aguamansa — La Caldera — Aguamansa: 3km/2mi; 1h; ● easy. Follow the main walk to the CRATER (❶), circle it, and return the same way.
Alternative start: ● Just after the 25min-point at ❶, take the first turn-off right, the steep, sign-posted **Camino de los Guanches** up to **Choza Chimoche** (❺), then return via the main walk.

Here's a short walk with plenty of variety — patches of forest, ravines, high and naked escarpments, shady moss-green paths, and some good views.

Start out at the TROUT FARM. From the main entrance (⭕), cross the road and walk uphill to the bus shelter. Follow the wide earthen path that heads up into the pines and heather directly behind the bus shelter (there may be a TRAIL BOARD here for the **PR TF 35**). A few minutes uphill, turn right on a narrower trail. You cross the access road to La Caldera in 15 minutes, then climb a bit more steeply to the recreation area itself. On reaching the tarred road that circles **La Caldera** (❶; **25min**), bear right; through the trees, you will see the crater *(la caldera)* below you on the left. There's a large parking area and bus stop.

Continue by circling the crater on the road. Ignore a first turn-off right. *(But turn right here on the Camino de los Guanches if you are following the 'Alternative start' above.)* Turn right on the next track (signed 'ZONA DE ACAMPADA'). *(But for the Short walk remain on the tarred road.)* Follow this track through slender pines and past the CAMPSITE (❷).

About 45 minutes uphill, a wide earthen trail strikes off to the

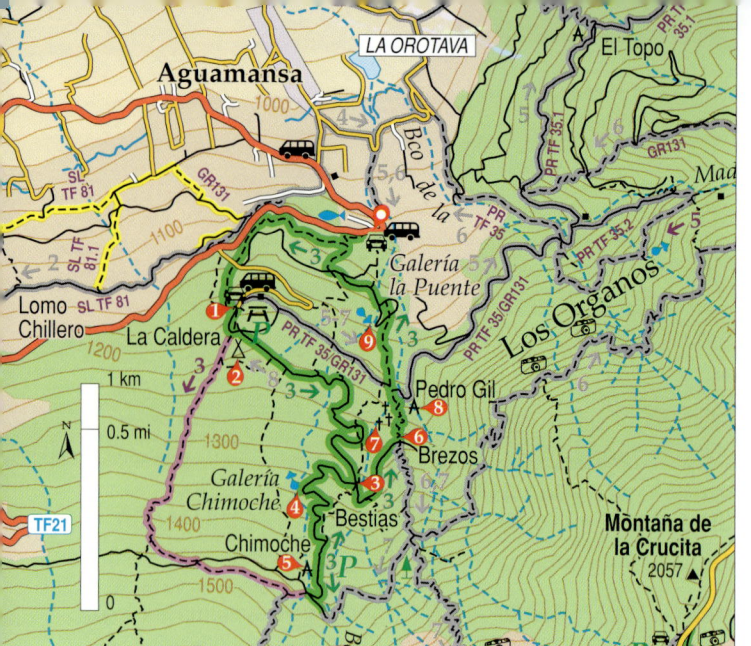

left at **Pasada de las Bestias** (**3**; the sign may be missing). You will return on that trail after visiting Choza Chimoche but, for now, be sure to *turn sharp right on the main track*. A small gorge lies below.

Beyond an enormous gravel deposit, you pass **Galería Chimoche** (**4**), a very important water source — as explained on page 44. Behind the two buildings, hidden in the rocky-faced embankment, is the *galería* ('water gallery' or tunnel). **Choza Chimoche** (**5**; **1h40min**; Picnic 3) sits in a sheltered hollow further up the track. Continue up the track at the left of the shelter for a few minutes, to an even lovelier picnic spot by the mouth of the **Barranco de Los Llanos**.

From this ravine retrace your steps for 20 minutes and head back to more garden-like surroundings. Turn off right at the **Pasada de las Bestias** T-junction (**3**) below Galería Chimoche. The track to the left is the route you climbed from La Caldera; you now head right on a wide earthen trail which skirts the ravine below. Five minutes from the turn-off you come to a small flat area called **Lomo de los Brezos** (**6**; **2h10min**). (The track ends just around the bend.)

From Lomo de los Brezos descend to the left on a path marked by a cairn. This path is called the '**Camino de las Crucitas**', named for the THREE LITTLE WOODEN CROSSES (**7**) shown opposite, standing on the left near the bottom of the path. From this serene spot, a forestry track is visible below on the right: it goes to Choza El Topo and Choza Almadi (Walk 5). You soon cross it at **Choza Pedro Gil** (**8**) — going straight ahead down a path shaded by tall heather, leafy trees, and the occasional pine. The trees are bearded with moss and lichen (photo on page 56).

Having crossed the track to **Galería La Puente** (**9**), your path rejoins the same track, which you follow to the left. A few minutes along, pass a track forking off to

Three little crosses sat at the bottom of the steep path down from Lomo de los Brezos, but they have been burnt out, as has the sturdy stone Pedro Gil shelter shown at the top — a no-go area in 2024. Pink-flowering cistus still brighten many of the mist-bound trails in the Orotava Valley, where the pines are bearded with moss.

the right. Some 200m/yds beyond it, you'll see your return path, also on the right. Two minutes downhill this path collides with a magnificent old pine that must be about 5m/15ft in circumference at the base of its trunk. Ignoring all the narrow side-paths, in five minutes you reach the main TF21 road and *BUS STOP* where you started out, at the main entrance to the *TROUT FARM* (**2h30min**).

Walk 4: AGUAMANSA • PINOLERE • LA FLORIDA

Distance: 4.5km/2.8mi; 1h15min
Grade: ● easy-moderate; steep descent of 550m/1800ft. *All on tar, but surprisingly popular*
Equipment: stout shoes, sunhat, fleece, rain-/windproof, picnic, water
Transport: 🚐 345 from Puerto to Aguamansa (Timetable 2); journey time 45min; alight at the 'El Velo' bus stop. Return on 🚐 373 from La Florida to La Orotava (not in the timetables; hourly departures at 20min past on weekdays; every 2 hours at 45 min past on weekends); journey time 10min; *change to* 🚐 345 (Timetable 2) or 353 (Timetable 3; journey to Puerto 20min
Alternative walk: Aguamansa — Choza Chimoche — La Florida: 13km/8mi; 3h25min. ● Moderate climb of 400m/1300ft and steepish (at times) descent of 900m/2950ft; access as Walk 3; equipment/return as above. Do Walk 3, then this walk.

Here's a perfect rural setting of peaceful farmlands. Bright-blooming flower beds enliven country cottages, wild fields are grazed under the watchful eyes of shepherds, ageing chestnuts stand guard over the declining slopes, and neat stone walls hide the season's produce.

Start out where you leave the bus at **Aguamansa** (⊙). Walk a few paces uphill and then turn left, steeply downhill, on a lane (just a few metres/yards below the Restaurante Aguamansa). After 200m/yds take the second right turn (Camino de Mamio). From here on you follow country roads.

Colour and greenery flow out of the landscape all the way. Hedges of white-flowering chimney broom *(escobón)* border the fields. Beyond a reservoir over to the left and a lane to the right, keep left at a JUNCTION (by a first SHRINE on the left; **20min**). Some 200m/yds further on, by the SHRINE (❶)

You pass a church on the left, the Ermita de Pinolere

This shrine is a landmark on both Walks 4 and 5. A farmer takes a break … Far left: colourful celebrations in Pinolere

shown above right, a lane comes in on the right (from Choza Perez Ventoso; Short walk 5). Keep straight on (left) here, ignoring a short-cut road to the right almost immediately.

Five minutes later, the road bends right just past houses 12 and 11b. You pass house 68 ('La Zarza'; ❷) and almost immediately turn right. This road eventually curves back 90° left and descends to a T-JUNCTION (**45min**). Turn left here, passing a RURAL LIFE MUSEUM (❸) with traditional stone and thatched buildings. At the next junction, by a CHURCH on the left, turn right downhill (small sign on the right: 'LA FLORIDA'). Keeping to the main road, continue down through **Pinolere**.

A good five minutes later, at a T-junction in **La Florida Alta** (❹; **1h**), turn left, ignoring a fork to the left immediately after. Cross straight over the main road beyond the SCHOOL in **La Florida**: the STOP FOR BUS 373 is just ahead, on the right (❺; **1h15min**).

Or turn left on the main road, against the one-way traffic, and continue for 15 minutes to a roundabout on the TF21. A BUS STOP (❻) is just along to the left.

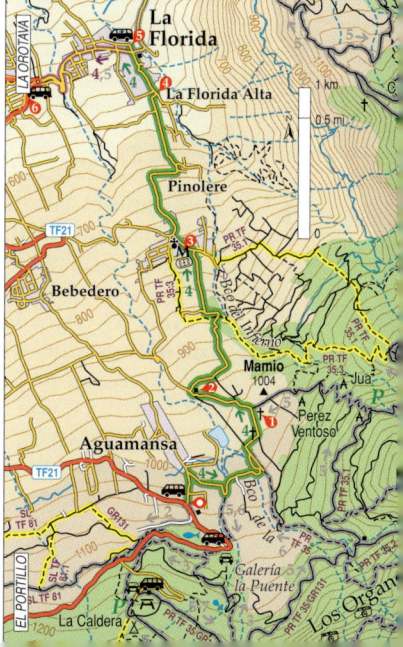

Walk 5: LA CALDERA • CHOZA EL TOPO • CHOZA ALMADI • PINO ALTO • LA FLORIDA

See also photos on pages 61, 62 and 63
Distance: 20km/12.5mi; 5h30min
Grade: ● a fairly strenuous full day's walk. It's easy, almost level walking to Choza El Topo, then a strenuous climb of 350m/1150ft to Choza Almadi, followed by a steep descent of 1000m/3300ft. *This hike is only suitable in good weather. There are only three shelters between La Caldera and Pino Alto, and temperatures can drop very suddenly on these heights (1200m/ 4000ft and above).*
Equipment: walking boots, sunhat, warm fleece, rain-/wind-proof, whistle, picnic, water
Transport: 🚌 345 from Puerto to La Caldera (Timetable 2); journey time 50min. Return as Walk 4 on pages 62-63.

Short walks
1 La Caldera — Choza El Topo — Choza Perez Ventoso — Aguamansa: 6km/3.7mi; 1h45min. ● Easy, with a slight ascent to Choza El Topo, then a steep descent of 200m/650ft to Choza Perez Ventoso (slippery when wet); access/return on 🚌 345 (Timetable 2); stout shoes or walking boots, sunhat, fleece, picnic, water. Follow the main walk to ❸ (1h), then descend the steep trail behind **Choza El Topo**. When you come to a wide track (with the ruined **Choza Inge Jua** above on the right), keep downhill. Asphalt soon comes underfoot, and **Choza Perez Ventoso** (also ruined) is on your left. Walk down to a junction with a SHRINE (❶) on your left and turn left. Follow this road (with walkers' signposts) to a T-junction in **Aguamansa**, then climb up left to the BUS STOP (❺) on the TF21.
2 La Caldera — Choza El Topo — Pinolere: At Llano de los Corrales (❹; 1h15min) you can chose to descend to **Pinolere** along PR TF 35.1 (7km/4.3mi; 3h; ● moderate) or PR TF 35.3 (6.5km/ 4mi; 2h30min; ● quite easy). Both trails are well signposted. From there pick up Walk 4.
3 Ruta del Agua: 6km/3.7mi; 2h15min. ● Grade/equipment/ access as main walk; same bus to return. Follow the main walk to the WATERHOUSE shown overleaf (❷; 35min), then turn right on the signposted, yellow/white way-marked PR TF 35.2, climbing the steep **Barranco Madre del Agua** by an old *canal*. On the descent you will pass an old *galería* off left with adjacent *canal* and distribution points. Rejoining the outward track, retrace your steps to La Caldera.

This walk requires a little energy, as you head up into cloud territory at about 1450m/4750ft. But wherever you pull up to rest, a panorama will unfold around you — if you beat the morning clouds. For most of the way, your views sweep along the whole Orotava Valley, from El Teide down to the ocean, and over to the western tip of the island. Grand specimens of indigenous pines will capture your attention. Out of cloud territory, you'll descend through terraced plots shaded by chestnut trees, a rural scene little changed by tourism. This is where I like to ponder, in the shade of a chestnut, and soak up the superb coastal view that lies before me.

Walk 5: From La Caldera to La Florida via Choza Almadi   65

The walk starts at **La Caldera** (⭕). Leaving the bus, take the road to the left. Follow the **PR TF 35/GR131** and then fork left on the **Pista de Mamio**, a forestry track signposted to *'LOS ORGANOS'*; it runs through heather and pines. Not far along, you cross a bridge straddling the end of a narrow ravine.

About **10min** along, various SIGNS appear; follow the main track around to the left, past **Choza Pedro Gil** (❶), shown on page 61. *(Walks 6 and 7 head south uphill at this point.)* In the sweeping U-shaped curve of the track, you'll notice a pine-covered slope. These tall and gracious trees look almost ornamental, with long wisps of pale green lichen hanging from their branches (see photos overleaf

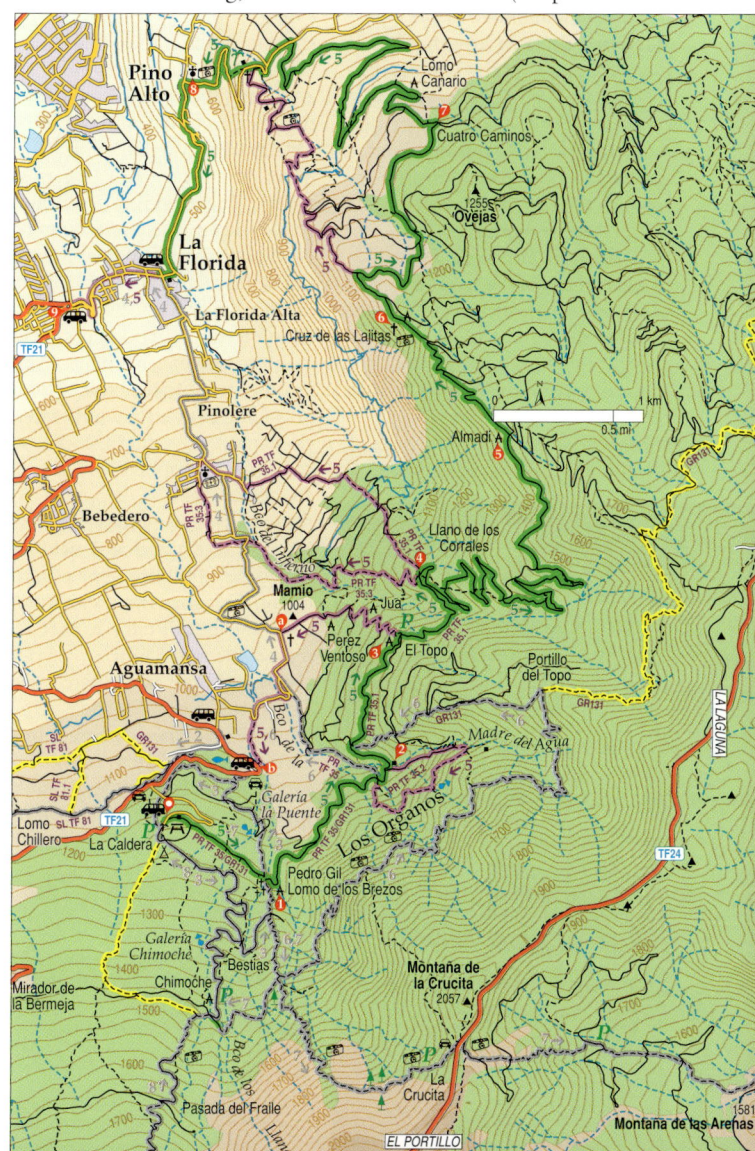

and on page 71). The highest farms in the valley, nestled in against the walls of the escarpment, lie a little below the track. Lower down, orchards can be seen through the pines. You pass the PR TF 35 descending left to Aguamansa and the PR TF 35.2 on the right (the 'RUTA DEL AGUA'). Two minutes later, the large stone **Casa del Agua (❷; 35min)**, built into the embankment at the **Barranco de la Madre del Agua**, is a focal point on the latter trail. *(Short walk 3 turns right here and returns via the trail passed two minutes back.)* Five minutes later, ignore a cairn-marked forestry track to the left, which *may* be signposted to Aguamansa.

Choza El Topo (❸; Picnic 5) is reached under **1h** from La Caldera. It's another good viewing spot for the Orotava Valley. Keep straight on along the Pista de Mamio beyond this shelter *(but for Short walk 1, descend the track behind the* choza*)*. Within the next 20 minutes, after crossing the **Barranco del Infierno**, the real ascent begins from **Llano de los Corrales (❹; 1h15min)**. *(Both versions of Short walk 2 descend from here to Pinolere.)*

Carved into the mountainside, the main walk track now zigzags lazily up towards Choza Almadi. It's a steady climb (there are some energy-sapping steep short-cuts). You may be swallowed up by clouds or mist as you approach the summit of the track, at 1450m/4750ft. The way curves back into an inner valley in the range, and then begins to descend out into the Orotava Valley again, with good views of the Los Organos mass of dissected rock. A little further along, the coastline unrolls.

Notice the dampness in the air. On cloudy days, all the plants are saturated with dew, giving rise to an interesting phenomenon: the majestic Canary pine plays a very important ecological role. The prevailing northerly winds carry clouds to the northern slopes, and create an atmosphere which causes condensation. The drippings from this moisture were measured over the period of a year and yield an incredible 2000 litres per square metre! This may not mean much to you — until I tell you that a reasonable rainfall for a year yields about 500 litres per square metre. This is the reason for the continuous planting of trees in bare or denuded areas of the forest: to feed the underground reservoirs (*galerías*) described on page 44.

You come to an intersection, where **Choza Almadi (❺; 2h**

The large Casa del Agua, where Short walk 3 turns up the Barranco de la Madre del Agua. Opposite: view to El Teide from the Orotava Valley

50min) sits below the track. Take a break here, before beginning the descent. Then turn left immediately and head straight downhill below the shelter. This descent is so steep that you'll find yourself almost leaning backwards! Some grand old trees tower overhead. At a fork two minutes down, you can take either branch (they rejoin); the upper fork to the left has better views. Now ignore all the many turn-offs to the right. Keep left all the way down to **Cruz de las Lajitas** (**6**; **3h15min**). There is a small white SHRINE to the left, buried in flowers, and a *choza*. The view over the Orotava Valley is superb.

From here keep to the main track, going straight downhill and ignoring any turn-offs. After about 10 minutes, at a signposted fork, go right.* At the next major junction a much-used, signposted 4-WHEEL-DRIVE CIRCUIT TRACK JOINS from the right. Continue straight ahead; now the gradient eases, and it's a fairly easy descent to a four-way junction, aptly called **Cuatro Caminos** (**7**). Turn left here on a track signposted 'LA CORUJERA' (it may also be signed to La Orotava, Pino Alto and/or Santa Ursula). Ignore a track off left (which *may* be signposted to La Orotava) and continue ahead. The track bends to the right and passes a small *choza* (**4h10min**). From here the track descends in long zigzags. When you reach a bend in the track with a tarmac lane going straight ahead, turn sharp back to the left, following the gravel track. The 4-WHEEL-DRIVE CIRCUIT LEAVES along the tarmac lane, and from now on you won't have to share the trail with vehicles. After about 10 minutes the track zigzags back right and a track joins from the left.

Soon a wire fence runs along on the left. Tarmac comes underfoot and you reach a T-junction with a narrow asphalt lane. Turn left and follow this lane towards Pino Alto. Watch for a track off left (the difficult route mentioned below left) and a SHRINE beside the road. Two minutes later (just past a house with a TALL LONE PALM TREE in its garden), you could take a three-minute short-cut on the right to cut a loop off the road.

Pino Alto appears, perched high above the rest of the valley. This typical Canarian village has a superb outlook. The CHURCH (**8**), with its grand balconied plaza, is an ideal place to get your breath back and absorb the view. Just beyond the church, turn left at a T-junction. The escarpment wall rises up protectively behind the village and, below, vineyards (which produce a white wine) cover most of the land. Following a steep descent and then a slight climb, you reach a junction at the beginning of **La Florida** (**5h 30min**). The STOP FOR BUS 373 (**9**) is just downhill to the right. Otherwise continue straight on for 15 minutes to the TF21 and turn left at the roundabout to the BUS STOP, for one of the frequent buses to Puerto.

---

*The sure-footed among you might like to use the map to take a more direct route to Pino Alto, but be warned: the route is very steep and slippery, with deep ruts (the track is used at weekends by locals with motorcycles, quad bikes, etc). The short-cut paths — where they still exist — are waymarked with faded yellow dots. *Don't attempt this route in wet conditions under any circumstances!*

Walk 6: THE ORGANOS 'HIGH ROAD': LA CALDERA • LOMO DE LOS BREZOS • AGUAMANSA

See also photos on pages 61, 66 and 67
Distance: 11km/6.8mi; 4h10min
Grade: ● ‼ strenuous climb of 400m/1300ft and descent of 500m/1650ft. You must be sure footed and have a head for heights. Although the walk is mostly well protected by chains and sturdy railings, there were still some exposed sections with no protection at time of writing
Equipment: walking boots, sunhat, warm fleece, rain-/windproof, picnic, water

Transport: 🚌 345 from Puerto to La Caldera (Timetable 2); journey time 50min, or 🚗. Return on 🚌 345 from Aguamansa — to Puerto (Timetable 2; journey time 45min), or back to your car at La Caldera

Shorter walk: La Caldera — spectacular chasm — La Caldera: 9km/5.6mi; 3h10min. ● ‼ Access, grade, equipment as above. Follow the main walk to ❸ (1h45min), then return the same way for 🚌 345 or your car.

Have you ever wondered what lies *above* Los Organos? This classic walk — one of the most popular trails in the Orotava Valley — will take you up into these cloud-catching peaks, where chasms of exuberant vegetation lie between fractured pinnacles. The route was closed for a few years (it is subject to frequent rock falls and landslips), but has recently been rebuilt and was in very good condition just before press date.

The walk starts at La Caldera (○; Picnic 6a). Follow Walk 5 to **Choza Pedro Gil** (**10min**), shown on page 61. Leave the GR131 here by taking the wide earthen path off right, signposted 'CAMINO A CANDELARIA'. (Walk 5 continues along the track.) The THREE (burnt out) LITTLE CROSSES you pass give this path its name: Camino de las Crucitas.

Fifteen minutes further uphill, at a small flat area (**Lomo de los Brezos**; ❶) you cross a track and follow the path slightly to the left, up the hillside. The way divides here and there, braiding itself up the slope. The side-on view of Los Organos and the eastern escarpment is quite impressive. It's hard to believe that the route winds up into those walls!

Ignore a path off to the right (**40min**). A few minutes later, turn left at a MAJOR JUNCTION (❷; **45min**), now taking the Organos 'high road'. *(Walk 7 turns right here, to make for La Crucita.)* Not far around the slope, you'll notice hundreds of small rosette plants (*Greenovia aurea*) on the rock face. Grey-green velvet-leafed bushes (*Sideritis* or 'Canarian edelweiss') will also catch your eye.

Greenovia aurea

You leave the Chimoche side of the slope and begin the long climb above Los Organos. You pass a VIEWPOINT at a rocky promontory and soon enter a plunging gorge, surrounded by precipitous, sharp peaks. Although the path is *very* exposed in places, sturdy railings allay any feelings of vertigo,

allowing you to enjoy the primeval setting.

At about **1h45min** you reach the END OF THE GORGE (**3**). *(The Shorter walk turns back here.)* Further on there is another fine VIEWPOINT — this one looking down to Aguamansa's trout farm, if the clouds aren't too low. Beyond this viewpoint the path progresses eastwards, zigzagging up and down across what seems inaccessible terrain. You swing into the enormous **Barranco de la Madre del Agua** (**4**), deep in the escarpment.

On leaving this valley and entering a wood, you soon find yourselves at the highest point in the route (**5**; **Portillo del Topo**, 1600m). As the GR131 continues contouring to the right, watch for your turn-off left on the red/white-waymarked **GR131**: this path heads down towards a large rocky 'hump' but, before reaching it, you descend a 'ramp' of rocks on the left side of the hump. At the bottom of the descent (**3h**) follow the path lined with stones on either side running alongside an old track.

Steps and another path take you down through the forest, now above the huge cleft of the Barranco de la Madre del Agua. On joining a TRACK COMING FROM CHOZA EL TOPO (**6**), follow it round the bend, ignoring a track off left. After just 10m/yds, turn left down another 'fairytale' path carpeted with pine needles. The bushes and trees are thickly bearded with wispy lichen.

Ten minutes downhill you meet the **Pista de Mamio** forestry track (**7**) followed in Walk 5. Straight across, a track marked with an 'X' twists and turns its way to Aguamansa. But you turn *left* here with the **PR TF 35**, in five minutes passing to the right of the large stone **Casa del Agua** shown on page 66, a focal point for highly recommended Short walk 5-3, the PR TF 35.2, the 'RUTA DEL AGUA'. Just past it, turn down right on a path signposted 'PR TF 35

View to Los Organos from La Caldera: it's very rare to see the 'organ pipes' through the mist! Right: lichen festoons the Canary pines all along the route.

AGUAMANSA' (**8**). Go straight on at the only junction. Tarmac comes underfoot, and then you come to a lane, which you follow to the left, rounding a bend. As you round a second bend in the lane, head left, following the fingerpost 'PR TF 35 CASA FORESTAL'.

Just over 10 minutes later you are on the TF21 in **Aguamansa** (**4h10min**), opposite the TROUT FARM, with its BUS STOP (**9**) two minutes to your left. The Aguamansa BUS SHELTER is five minutes to the right, past Restaurante Aguamansa. Rooftops weighed down with vividly-coloured hanging plants and roadside planters brimming with flowers are your last memories of this walk.

Walk 7: THE CANDELARIA TRAIL: LA CALDERA • LA CRUCITA • ARAFO

See also photos on pages 11, 58-59, 61, 71
Distance: 12.5km/7.8mi; 5h
Grade: ● very strenuous, with a steep climb (800m/2600ft) and steep *gravelly* descent (1500m/4950ft)
Equipment: walking boots, sunhat, warm fleece, rain-/windproof, long trousers, whistle, picnic, water
Transport: 🚌 345 from Puerto to La Caldera (Timetable 2); journey time 50min. Return on 🚌 121 from Arafo to Santa Cruz (not in the timetables): departs Arafo at 40min past the hour until 20.45 (hourly Mon-Fri; at 10min past every *second* hour Sat, Sun, holidays); journey time 50min; *change to* 🚌 100/102/103 to Puerto (Timetable 1); journey 1h

Short walk: La Caldera — Choza Chimoche — La Caldera: 5.5km/3.5mi; 1h45min. ● Easy-moderate climb/descent of 300m/1000ft; equipment as above, but stout shoes will suffice. In company with the main walk, follow Walk 6 (page 69) to the MAJOR JUNCTION met at 45min (**❷**). Keep right here. Just uphill from the junction, below the large pine, bear right on a path (the main walk heads to the left of the pine). The path ends at the **Barranco de los Llanos** (**ⓐ**; 55min); follow the forestry track downhill a couple of minutes, to **Choza Chimoche** (**ⓑ**). Descend the track behind the shelter, picking up Walk 8 at its 4h15min-point at waypoint **❼**, page 78, to descend to **La Caldera**.

This hike follows an old pilgrims' way known as the Candelaria Trail. It originally began at La Orotava. It climbs the steep escarpment of the central massif and then twists endlessly down to the sea at Candelaria. Today, the land between Arafo and Candelaria is so built-up that the few pilgrims who still make the journey leave the trail at our destination, Arafo. The Virgin of Candelaria is Tenerife's patron saint, whose Assumption is celebrated each year on August 14-15th. This long, but gratifying walk offers superb panoramas, encompassing corners of immense beauty.

Walk 7: The Candelaria Trail

Start out by following **Walk 6** (page 69) from **La Caldera** (●) up to the MAJOR JUNCTION (❷; **45min**), where Walk 6 heads left: here turn *right*. Barely a minute up, at a FORK, the main path veers off round the right-hand side of the ridge. You do *not*! At this point you are just below a large pine: continue up the ridge, to the left of the pine. *(The path to the right leads to Chimoche and is the Short walk route.)* For the first few minutes of the climb, you are in a sunken path. A couple of minutes up, ignore a path branching off to the left. The route will eventually take you up and over the *cumbre*.

As the climb steepens, more of the valley becomes visible through the sparse pine growth. Some 25 minutes from the last turn-off, on a bend, you look over into a strip of bare *barranco* that emanates a soft mixture of pinks, mauves, browns and greys. Seconds up, your path briefly runs alongside the DYKE (❸) shown overleaf. The vegetation undergoes a change here: small bushes of Canarian edelweiss (*Sideritis*) turn white as their velvety leaves catch the sun, and scraggy chimney broom (*escobón*) and *retama* take control of the slope. The path is so colourful that it's easy to forget the wider landscapes on view.

All the way up, the vast view stretches across the upper inclines of the Orotava Valley, where more and more land is being given over to buildings. At **1h35min** you find yourselves sheltered between a low DYKE (❹) and a few pines. A faded arrow points you through a gap in this natural rock wall. From here, you can see the path heading across the escarpment. Another patch of writing on rocks, and a WHITE ARROW pointing left, are your next landmarks. The path climbs steeply through rocks and over stones in a multi-coloured volcanic landscape. A good look-out point lies midway between the dyke and the TF24 above.

When you reach **La Crucita** (❺; **2h20min**; Picnic 7) at an altitude of 1980m/6500ft, get out your anchor! From here on it's down, down, as you descend the southern escarpment. Cross the TF24 and, 50m/yds along to the left, turn right on a forestry track. The isolated valley you are about to enter lies far below. The entrance to the valley is blocked by an enormous naked black mound, Las Arenas. You have the stupendous view shown on page 11: dark, pine-sprinkled slopes drop down to a coastal plain tessellated in faded browns and greens. The sea stretches out into the distance.

Three minutes (250m/yds) down the track, your PATH (❻) strikes off to the left and slithers its way down the stark slope. Large WOODEN PEGS stand on either side of the path. These will be your path waymarkers until you reach Las Arenas. The descent will be at a snail's pace: there's loose gravel under foot, and the slope looks almost vertical. Within minutes, you cross the track. Turn left: your continuation is 10m/yds downhill, on the right. Soon you head back into pines, under which *codéso* and

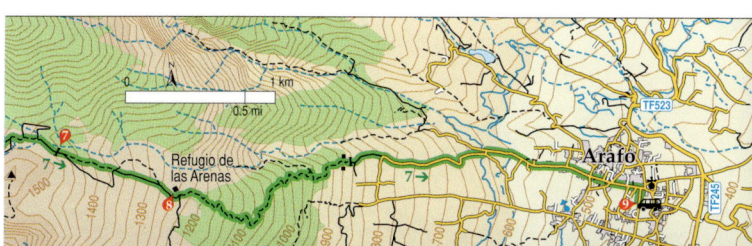

broom shelter. The path forks just above the track. If you fork right, along the crest of the ridge, the stretch is vertiginous, but railings help part of the way. (An alternative is to fork left to the track, then turn right.) Where the main (crest) path rejoins the track by a CAIRN, continue downhill for 20m/yds, then take the path on the

Walk 7: The Candelaria Trail

left, on a bend. It squiggles through the trees, past lovely picnic spots on relatively flat land and, at the edge of the wood, with spectacular views (another setting for Picnic 7). Where the path is faint, keep the shallow ravine on the left within sight, and you're sure to be okay. Sporadic small dots of red paint help you along.

Recross the track once more, and again find the path slightly below and to the left. At the next track crossing, find the ongoing path a few metres downhill to the left. A minute downhill finds you in a shallow *barranco:* descend this for a couple of minutes, then swing out of the ravine and around the hillside.

Smooth black sand soon comes underfoot. The outline of a rounded volcanic hill completely disrupts the landscape as it appears through the trees. You come face-to-face with this bulging black monster, **Montaña de las Arenas**, at **3h15min**. It obliterates everything. The track is not far below; shortly, you rejoin it. Follow it downhill for about a minute; then, on the next bend, cut off right across the sand. On meeting the track again, leave it after two minutes — just past a METAL GATE (**7**): take the path that veers straight ahead off the track, and keep alongside the ravine. (The track heads slightly away from the ravine, to the right, at this point.) Gran Canaria is on the horizon. Arafo, your destination, is far below, and the immediate landscape reveals an intriguing beauty: chestnut trees are the sole survivors in these black sands. Bent and crippled, these 'triffid' creatures have never managed to raise their backs. It's a unique sight.

Some seven minutes later, when you next meet the track (on a bend), follow it downhill. In ten minutes you reach the simple stone **Refugio de las Arenas** (**8**) that the pilgrims visit. To continue, head to the bend in the track just below the refuge and take the small path down to the left (CAIRN), briefly encountering scrub and bushes.

Scrubland is eventually replaced by a Canary pine forest, and you pass some proud old specimens. The way (always marked with CAIRNS) splinters and rejoins. In just over 600m/0.4mi the path swings left across the hillside and, a few minutes later, heads right, soon crossing an old (probably dry) *canal*. Five minutes below the *canal*, you come to the edge of the forest. Again you wind your way through scrub.

Meeting a narrow lane just beyond two WATERHOUSES and a chain barrier (Camino Mora del Estanque; **4h25min**), follow it straight ahead for just under 1km. Here you turn left for a mere 20m/yds to another lane (Camino la Canal Alta), where you go right. The lane, now called Calle Eduardo Curbelo Fariña, heads straight to the main square in **Arafo** (**9**; Plaza La Iglesia; **5h**). The BUS STATION (ESTACIÓN DE GUAGUAS) is 150m to the right along Avenida Reyes de España.

Left: at 1h the path runs alongside a dyke.

Walk 8: EL PORTILLO • CORRAL DEL NIÑO • CHOZA CHIMOCHE • LA CALDERA

See also photos on pages 67, 71, 80-81, 96
Distance: 17km/10.5mi; 5h
Grade: ● moderate but long, with an ascent of 250m/820ft at the start and a fairly steep descent of 1000m/3300ft. The first part of the walk, after leaving the road, is along National Park Trail No. 21; below Montaña del Limón it's along Park Trail No. 34.
Equipment: walking boots, sunhat, warm fleece, rain-/windproof, picnic, water
Transport: 🚌 348 from Puerto to El Portillo (Timetable 5); journey time 1h. Return on 🚌 345 from La Caldera to Puerto (Timetable 2); journey time 50min
Alternative start: This adds 3km/2mi; 1h to the route, but cuts out what some hikers may find a boring road walk. *Note that not all of this route is shown on our maps.* Cross the road from the **Portillo** INFORMATION CENTRE and follow Walk 9, but fork left after five minutes on **National Park Path No. 2** and follow this as it winds uphill. After about an hour take a path swinging east across a wide desolate plain (where Path No. 2 goes right rejoin Walk 9). Towards the end of the plain the path gets fainter, but if you veer to the right, towards some bushes, it becomes clear again and within a minute you reach a bulldozed track. Turn left (north) and follow this to the TN24 road. Turn right and in 15 minutes you are at **Corral del Nino** (❶).

A rolling landscape of perfectly-rounded volcanic mounds, mellow, glistening slopes, and the occasional chirp of calling birds sets this walk apart from the others. Over an hour on an asphalt road does not sound like a very appealing beginning to a walk. But the TF24 is not a busy road, except on weekends (or you could try the Alternative start above). The striking natural beauty of the landscape, and the omnipresent El Teide, detract from the little traffic encountered.

On your bus ride up to El Portillo, you'll pass the Piedra La Rosa — the basaltic rock formation in the shape of a rose shown on page 57. You may also see piles of pine needles by the road, awaiting collection. They're used as packing material for easily-bruised fruit.

Start out in front of the RESTAURANT at **El Portillo** (⭕): head east on the La Laguna road (TF24). **Montaña de Guamaso** will be your first significant landmark, on your left. It's the focal point for Walk 14 in the national park's numbering scheme. Along the roadside, the white and yellow blooms of *margarita del Teide*, *retama* and Canary flaxweed prove their worth in springtime. The road climbs some 250m/820ft to Corral del Niño. Being just outside the perimeter of the crater, it is not exactly like the landscape of Las Cañadas (Walk 9) — it lacks the aggressive sharpness. There's a

Walk 8: From El Portillo to La Caldera 77

smooth, flowing undulation here. As you progress, El Teide becomes complete behind you, and there are wide-ranging views of the Orotava Valley on cloudless days. The weird white buildings of the observatory on Izaña catch your attention.

In under **1h10min**, just before the 'Corral del Niño' SIGN (**1**), turn off left on a wide track. It takes you into a rolling sea of colours. The sun catches all the hidden tones as you follow the contours. You're crossing a giant palette, as you head down towards the pines far below. Pebble-sized scoria covers much of the land, and volcanic mounds rise like giant anthills.

An hour down the track brings you the point where it makes a hairpin loop to the left: take the signposted, well-defined short-cut path off left (**2**; **2h10min**). Rejoining the track in two minutes, turn left. Barely one minute along (some 75m/yds), head right on your continuing path, hedged in by *retama*. From a PASS (**3**), the burgundy-red slopes of **Montaña del Limón** soon comes into view on your right. This small volcanic mound makes a popular walk from La Caldera; a path to its east allows for a good circuit.

The forest begins rather shyly, with small scattered pines. The path zigzags symmetrically down to the track at '**Cumbrita Fria**' (**4**; **2h50min**; *the sign may be missing*), where you turn right. You'll see plants with twigs like bottle-brushes, called *codéso* (see drawing on page 129). During the winter, they're just a pleasing green, but in spring they enliven the landscape with their brilliant yellow blossoms.

Some 20 minutes downhill, on a bend, you pass a fork off to the left; around 10 minutes later, you leave the main track to turn off to the right for Choza Chimoche: a CAIRN waymarked '**Cuevitas del Limón**' (**5**) marks the turn-off. (The main track continues left to the Ramón el Caminero picnic site and the TF21, an hour's walk away.)

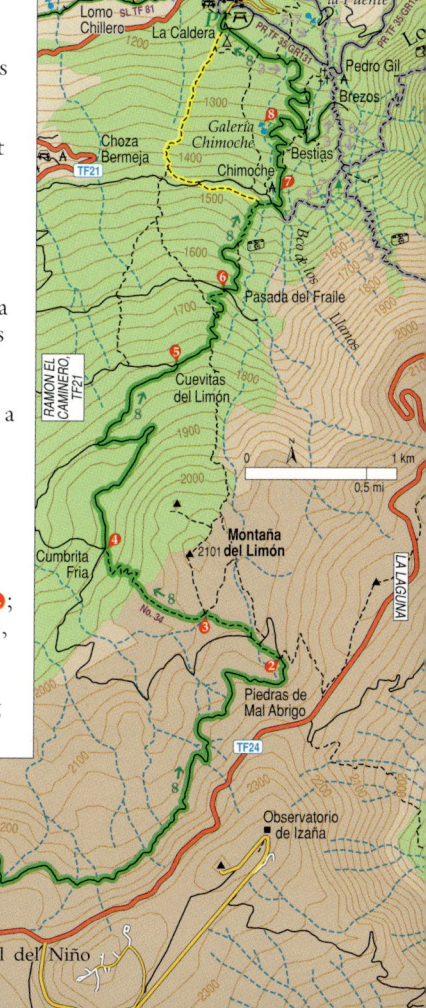

The track now steepens considerably. You cross another forestry track at **Pasada del Fraile** (**6**). Not far above Choza Chimoche, the track ends, and a path brings you to the *choza*. If forestry work confuses the route, always keep right, near the beautiful ravine on your right.

Facing **Choza Chimoche** (**7**; **4h15min**), the continuation to La Caldera is the second (descending) track to the right, the **Camino de los Guanches**. (The first track to the right climbs to the Barranco de los Llanos.) You swing behind the shelter, dipping into a small flat area — a very picturesque spot for a picnic. After descending for a little over 10 minutes, the track passes **Galería Chimoche** (**8**). A few minutes later, keep left downhill at a T-JUNCTION, to reach **La Caldera** and the BUS STOP (**9**; **5h**).

Views to El Teide, just beyond Montaña del Limón

Walk 9: LAS CAÑADAS

See the map pages 82-83; see also photos on pages 21, 22-23 and 92-93
Distance: 18km/11.2mi; 4h45min
Grade: ● easy ascent of 200m/650ft; short descent. But moderate on account of the *length*. All National Park Trail No. 4.
NB: there is only one bus a day.
Equipment: stout shoes, long trousers *and* shorts, gloves, warm fleece, rain-/windproof, sunhat, picnic, water
Transport: 🚌 348 (Timetable 5) from Puerto to El Portillo (journey time 1h). Return from the Parador de las Cañadas (journey time 2h)
Short walk: Montaña de Majuá — Piedras Amarillas — Parador de las Cañadas: 8.4km/5.2mi; 2h20min. ● Easy; equipment and access as above, but leave the bus at the El Teide cable car stop and return from the *parador*. From the cable car bus stop, return to the TF21 and continue south towards Montaña de Majuá, the large brown mound on the left. Three minutes along, turn off on the track heading towards it. This is **National Park Trail No. 16**. First climb to the top of **Montaña de Majuá** (**❶**), then continue along the track. Ignore all turn-offs — *especially at areas near beehives, signed 'Peligro, Colmenas' (danger, bees)*. An intriguing volcanic landscape unfolds. Some 55 minutes along the track, you come upon some little houses hidden in the rock — the '**Sanatorio**' (**❷**), where more than 100 tuberculars lived at the start of the 20th century. A good 10 minutes later, you pass through a barrier, soon meeting the Las Cañadas track followed in the main walk. Turn right along it and pick up the main walk at **❹** (the 3h30min-point); the *parador* (**❻**) is 50min away.

F ew people will ever walk on the moon, but this ramble inside Tenerife's great volcanic crater, Las Cañadas, must be a close approximation of the weird and awesome lunar landscape. (The *cañadas* are plains of sedimentary rock or gravel — and you will see seven of them on this hike — but the name 'Las Cañadas' is commonly applied to the crater in which these plains lie.) Tenerife has been a bed of volcanic activity for millennia. In fact, this activity is responsible for far more change on the island than are the elements. Controversy still exists about how the great crater of Las Cañadas was formed (the caption on page 23 will give you some idea of its immensity). One opinion claims that it is an enormous depression: Las Cañadas was originally covered by a dome. The collapse of the dome created the double crater which makes up this gigantic cauldron — the western side below the Roques de García and the eastern side stretching back to El Portillo. The other theory claims that erosion and the elements cut a large valley, opening to the north, and that this valley was later filled in by the surging up of El Teide and its off-sider, Pico Viejo. In either case, the crater was created some 200,000 years ago. The most recent activity here was a mere 200 years ago, when Pico Viejo blew its top.

Piedras Amarillas

Start at **El Portillo**'s CAÑADAS VISITORS' CENTRE () and take the gravel track opposite, signposted 'SIETE (SEVEN) CAÑADAS' (Trail No. 4 in the national park's numbering scheme). The track quickly disappears into turbulent terrain and spilled masses of sharp rock. In **5min**, ignore Trail No. 2 forking to the left and walk round a barrier (for vehicles). There are no turn-offs on this walk; you remain alongside the crater walls for nearly the whole hike. But at this point the walls on your left are rather insignificant, and it's not yet obvious that you're inside a crater. Smooth and perfectly-shaped scoria cones testify to former volcanic activity. The subtly-coloured *cañadas* give a touch of the desert. In winter these shallow gravelly plains often fill with water from melting snow.

As the track makes its way towards the escarpment, the perfectly-formed volcanic cone of **Montaña Mostaza** is seen ahead to the right. Further along, a beautiful tall wine-coloured rock formation appears in the wall itself. Some time later, you pass more interesting rock formations surrounded by beds of loose gravel; Japanese rock gardens come to mind. Then you descend to the **Cañada de las Pilas** (❶; **2h**), a long gravel 'lake' with 'islands' of rock.

Half an hour later, having crossed a small crest, you look across the large expanse of the even more impressive **Cañada de la Grieta** (❷; **2h30min**). Small crumbling animal pens sit in sheltered corners of the rock, a reminder of the days when the *cañadas* were grazed. A feeling of

desolation hangs over the place, but in spring the *taginaste rojo*, the 'Pride of Tenerife' (see page 2), cheers the slopes on the left with its conical tower of close-knit red blooms.

The large flat-topped peak that has been shadowing you around the last few bends is **Guajara**, and you soon pass the turn-off left for the ascent (③). Ignore the track off right (④; **3h45min**) to Montaña de Majuá and the Teide cable car. *(The Short walk comes in here.)* Next the bizarrely-sculpted **Piedras Amarillas** (⑤) catch the eye; this is an unsurpassed viewing point for the western side of the crater. Beyond these rocks you join a tarred road and leave the park. Just past the park barrier, take the

In the Cañadas, with Montaña de Guajara in the distance and margaritas del Teide *in the foreground*

short-cut track on the right. The **Parador de las Cañadas** (⑥; **4h45min**), has a café where you can swap experiences with dozens of walkers while you await the bus.

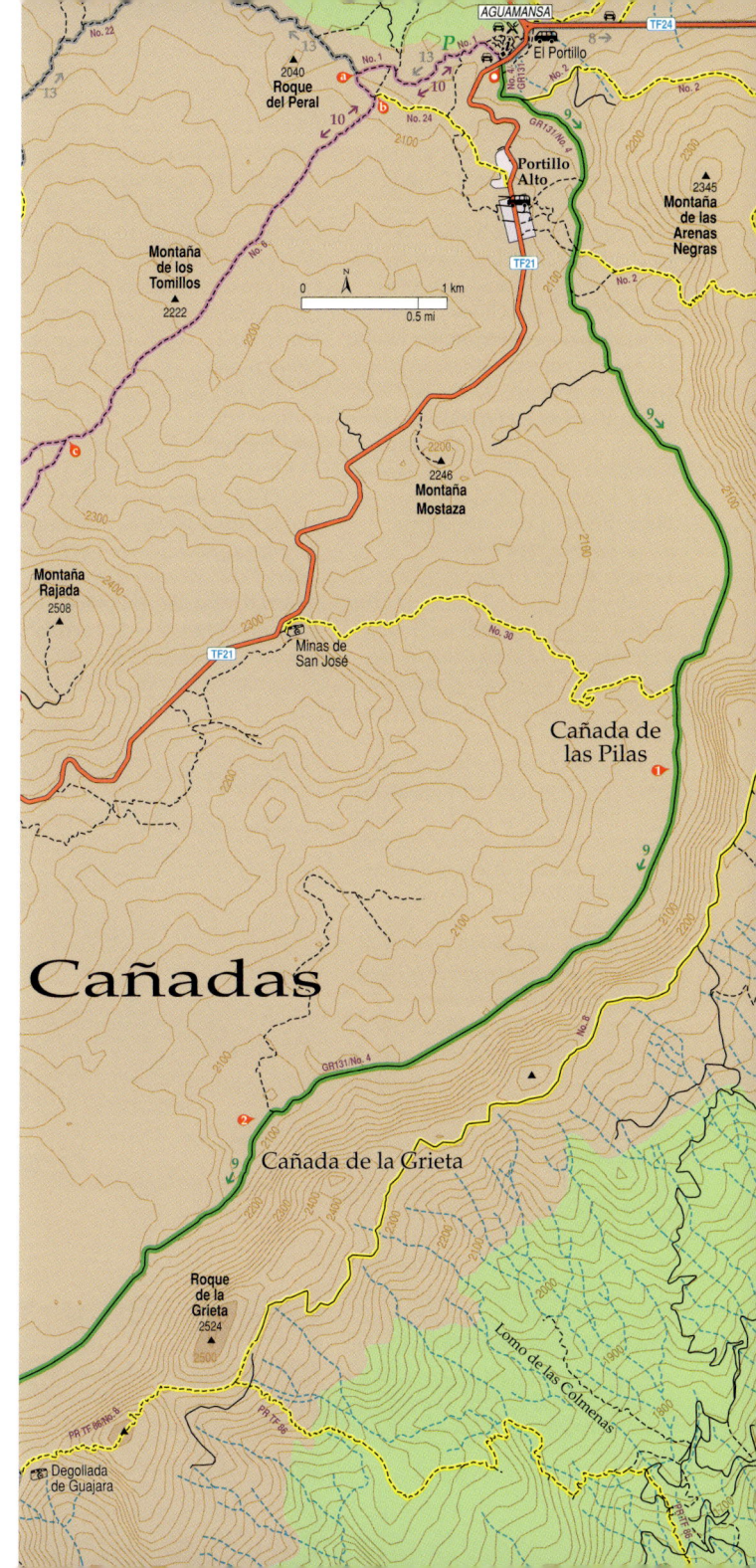

Walk 10: EL TEIDE

See the map on pages 82-83
Distance: 9.5km/5.9mi; 4h50min *for the ascent;* 18.5km/11.5mi; 7h45min *return.*
NB: You must have a (free) permit to climb the final 150m/yds to the summit of El Teide, a protected area. It's easiest to book online: see **reservasparquesnacionales.es** and click on 'English'. Otherwise you could go in person to the national park offices in La Orotava: C/Sixto Perera González, No. 25. Either way you must present your passport (or a scan) and stipulate a two-hour time slot for your arrival: *allow up to a good 6h!*
Grade: ● *very strenuous* ascent and descent of 1367m/4485ft; the path is good. *Take this walk very seriously: problems can include altitude sickness, no drinking water en route, and finding both the Refugio de Altavista and the cable car station at the summit closed.* The cable car *(teleférico)* may stop running *at any time* due to strong winds, in which case you'll have to descend on foot. Be prepared! Pay particular attention to the weather. Summer is obviously the best time for this hike (but be on the hill by dawn). *In winter don't attempt it if there is even the most remote chance of bad weather.* I describe the walk as a one-way ascent to the summit and return by cable car — harder on the lungs, but easier on the legs. The best way to tackle this hike, however, is to climb to the Refugio de Altavista and spend the night there. Early in the morning, make the final ascent to catch the sunrise. The *refugio* is *usually* open all year, but it is closed at present. When it reopens, reservations will be *essential* (see **volcanoteide.com**

for full details). Meanwhile, there is a bivouac area: see the permit website. The walk starts on National Park Trail No. 7 and finishes with Trails 10 (for which the permit is needed), 11 and 12.
Equipment: walking boots, warm fleece, windproof, sunhat, gloves, long trousers, thick socks, picnic, *plenty of water*
Transport: 🚌 348 from Puerto to/from the Montaña Blanca turn-off (Timetable 5); journey time 1h35min, or 🚗: park at KM40 on the TF21. *There is no time to travel both ways by bus. Arrange for friends/taxi to take you to the start of the walk or collect you.*
Alternative walk: El Portillo — Montaña Blanca — El Portillo: 20km/12.4mi; 5h15min. ● Moderate-strenuous, with an ascent

Two fit runners descending from Teide's summit. From up here, you really can *believe this is Spain's highest mountain.*

Walk 10: El Teide 85

of 700m/2100ft; equipment as above; access as Walk 13 and return on the same bus, or 🚗 to/from El Portillo. Follow Walk 13 (page 95) to its 20min-point, where it turns right. Turn *left* here (**a**) and, at a JUNCTION (**b**) three minutes later, turn right. Now refer to the map to fork right at **c**, join the main walk at **2**, follow it to **3**, and rise to the summit of **Montaña Blanca** (**d**; 2h40min). From here return down the track past where you joined it at **2**, then take the first track off left (at **1**, about 20min down). 50m/yds along, go left on a path (**e**). You rejoin your outgoing route at **c** in 30 minutes.

El Teide is the result of numerous volcanic eruptions. Pico Viejo, to the west of El Teide, was probably the most significant, and El Pilón (the peak itself) is still active. El Pilón rose over an older and much larger crater called La Rambleta, which lies just to the left of the cable car station near the summit. There are not many high volcanic mountains where one can begin the assault at well over halfway up, but we start this climb at the 2350 metre-mark. Another plus is that you needn't be a mountaineer to tackle this hike: from bottom to top, there's an easy-to-follow path.

*But you must be **very fit**.* Among the problems you may

encounter is altitude sickness — the signs usually being nausea and a headache. This often results when ascending too quickly. A slower ascent, with frequent rests, may relieve your sickness but, if it persists, it's best to turn back.

Start out at the TURN-OFF TO MONTAÑA BLANCA AT KM40 (**O**). Follow the track towards Montaña Blanca. The ascent of El Teide is No. 7 in the national park's scheme, so you will see small plaques with that number along the way. The landscape here — blanketed in pumice and scoria, interrupted by the occasional patch of jagged rock, wallows in desolation.

Some **10min** from the bus stop ignore a track off right (**1**; Trail No. 27, the return route for the Alternative walk). In **20min** you pass two short-cut paths to the left, but they are closed to walkers (again for conservation reasons). As you rise up, don't forget to look back at the unique view. In the Cañadas lie what look like rough mounds of chocolate. The walls clearly delineate the limits of the crater. The visitors' centre is but a few daubs of white.

In **35min** Trail No. 6, the route of the Alternative walk from El Portillo, comes in from the right (**2**), and eventually (**1h20min**) you come to an OLD CAR PARK (**3**; 2750m/9000ft), just below the summit of **Montaña Blanca**. For those ascending El Teide, this is where the real climbing begins. A park notice board stands at the foot of the sandy path, which is clear throughout. From down here, the side of El Teide seems to be split vertically: the left is clothed in dark lava flow and the right in light crusty pumice.

At **2h35min** the **Refugio de Altavista** (**4**) is no longer a dot on the mountainside. You're there,

3270m/10,725ft up. Hopefully, you are spending the night here and continuing the climb before daybreak. If so, be sure to read up about what to expect at the refuge and what to take with you at www.volcanoteide.com.

The onward path continues up behind the shelter, to the left, through a landscape covered in stones and chunks of rock. Less than 20 minutes up from Altavista, turn off right for the **Cueva del Hielo** (**5**), a minute away (the turn-off is marked by a small pile of stones and usually a signpost). Snow used to be packed in this large sunken pit, to make ice for medicinal and other purposes. Unless it it cordoned off, a springy metal ladder allows entry to this den: *take care!* Inside the cave are many stalactites.

Returning to the main path, the smooth volcanic cone of Montaña Mostaza (Walk 9) stands out below. Soon the walk levels out a bit. If a wind is blowing, as it often is, this is where it will be in full force. You quickly come to a T-junction, where you turn right to the **Mirador de la Fortaleza** (**6**). After enjoying the view over the Orotava Valley, return to the main path and keep right.

The way becomes a paved path twisting through a wild sea of rock. It takes you past the path to the summit, straight to the CABLE CAR STATION/BAR (**7**; **3h25min**). Rising puffs of steam betray concealed holes in the ground. Whiffs of sulphur waft by. If your hands need warming, hold them over these steaming holes. The

Volcanic bombs ('Teide's Eggs') are strewn across Montaña Blanca. Right: remember that the cable car only runs in fine weather!

drop in temperature causes small droplets of condensation, and strings of frozen water crystallise on the rocks; when the sun's rays catch these droplets, the slope appears diamond-studded.

To climb to the peak, show your permit to one of the park rangers and return to the ascent path. It's a further 20 minutes to the SUMMIT (**8**; **3h45min**). A small crater (80m/yds diameter) lies just below the peak. Here the soft colours of an ice cream parlour surround you: banana, peach melba, strawberry, mocha, pistachio. On a clear day, your view encompasses four islands — La Gomera, Gran Canaria, El Hierro and La Palma.

Before boarding the cable car for the return, follow the path that heads below the station. A 20-minute walk takes you to the **Mirador de Pico Viejo** (**9**; **4h40min**), for a perfect view over this massive crater (800m diameter!), before you head back to the bar (**4h50min**).

If you are returning to the TF21 on foot, retrace your steps, allowing just under three hours for the descent (**7h45min**).

Walk 11: ROQUES DE GARCIA AND LA CATEDRAL

Distance: 4km/2.5mi; 1h25min
Grade: ● moderate, with ascents of 150m/500ft overall (the final ascent is steep and slippery). National Park Trail No. 3
Equipment: walking boots, sunhat, fleece, rain-/windproof, gloves, picnic, water
Transport: 🚌 348 from Puerto to/from the Parador de Las Cañadas (Timetable 5); journey time 2h; or 🚗: park at the Mirador de la Ruleta, opposite the *parador* (28° 13.399'N, 16° 37.822'W)

This hike has got to be the gem of Las Cañadas. It's short, it's very accessible, and it's a geological treat. But be prepared for lots of company on this circuit round the Roques (Picnic 11). Before starting the walk, climb to the **Mirador de la Ruleta**, a fine viewpoint overlooking the Cañada Llano de Ucanca. The gigantic fractured rock rising up in front of you, out of this *cañada*, is called La Catedral. You'll walk in its shadow on the return leg of the hike. This is a waymarked walk (Trail No. 3 in the national park scheme), so you'll see small plaques with this number.

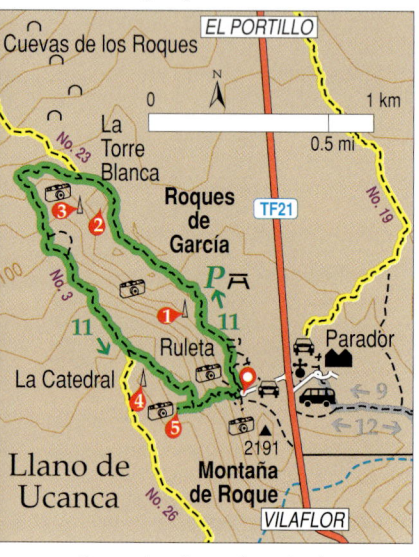

Returning from the *mirador*, **start out** by following the designated path heading north from the ROUNDABOUT (⊙), alongside the eroded rocks. The dramatic, solitary rock pillar on your left, featured in all the brochures, is

Roque Chinchado rises above walkers as they start to round the Roques de García, in full view of El Teide

Walk 11: Roques de García and La Catedral

Roque Chinchado (❶). Soon you come to another good lookout point. From here your path is bordered by stones. The path narrows as it passes between a ridge of rough, jagged rock on the right and the *roques* on the left.

Lumps of *pahoehoe* lava begin rising up around you as you approach the **Roques Blancos** (❷), the last of the Roques de García. The lava flow is usually a smooth stream of distorted, rolling hillocks and hollows; parts of it resemble cord, or coils of rope — hence the name. The ropey lava flow is formed on the thin crust of the stream, either by the movement of liquified lava underneath, or by the sliding of the crust where it has thrust up into a hillock. The more common lava up here is the 'A-A' (block lava) — large scoriaceous masses of jagged, fragmented rock.

La Torre Blanca (❸; the White Tower) is a solitary rock met at the **25min**-mark. North of here are many caves, the **Cuevas de Los Roques** (now out of bounds to walkers, due to damage to plants and the ropey lava). These caves were formed millennia ago when the surface crust thickened but the lava underneath continued to run, spreading its tentacles. When these streams subsided, they left an extensive

Before starting the walk proper, join the crowds climbing to the Mirador de la Ruleta.

network of tunnels and caves — some of them extending up to 1000m/3300ft back into the slope!

Continuing on the circuit, you quickly reach a 'balcony' *mirador* offering a last look over the lake-sized Cañada Llano de Ucanca. From here cairns mark your descent towards the *cañada*. The path swings back to the left and you circle behind the rocks. Rocks of all dimensions rear up before you — jagged upthrusts ... sheets of rock ... twisted fingers. Note, too, the 'waterfall' of ropey lava that pours through a gap in the rocks. Look back! With the ever-present El Teide in the background, and the pastel-coloured rocks in the foreground, you won't be able to put your camera away. A spectrum of volcanic hues saturates the landscape. If you're lucky enough to catch the *retama* in bloom, the view is even more spectacular.

Soon you're in the shadow of the imposing rock, **La Catedral** (❹). Rising over 100m/330ft from the plain, with rocky spire-like pinnacles, it is well named. Here the hard work begins: you have to climb straight up to the car park — a 25-minute slog. (When the path splits in two, both branches end at the same place, but the route to the left is easier; the path to the right is steep with a lot of loose shale.) Along the way, a slight detour to a MASSIVE ROCK (❺) on the right affords another fine view over the **Llano de Ucanca**, before you return to the CAR PARK (**1h25min**).

Walk 12: MONTAÑA DE GUAJARA

See also photos on pages 80, 88-89 and 90
Distance: 10.3km/6.4mi; 4h30min
Grade: ● moderate-strenuous climb and descent of 650m/2130ft. The ascent is quite easy, and the newly engineered descent path is clear and without exposure. Still, the walk is not recommended in unsettled weather. National Park Trails Nos. 4, 5, 15 and 31.
Equipment: walking boots, sunhat, fleece, windproof, long trousers, gloves, thick socks, picnic, water
Transport: 🚌 348 from Puerto to/from the Parador de las Cañadas (Timetable 5); journey time 2h; or 🚗: park at the *parador* (28° 13.422'N, 16° 37.674'W)

Shorter walk: *parador* — Degollada de Guajara — *parador*: 8.5km/5.3mi; 2h40min. ● Easy-moderate climb and descent of under 250m/820ft; access and equipment as above. Follow the main walk to ❺ (1h30min); return the same way.

Guajara is Tenerife's third highest mountain, standing at 2717m/8910ft. This is an easy, straightforward climb, offering superb views down into the crater of Las Cañadas. As you ascend Guajara's back, the southern coastal plain unravels in a haze below. After taking a break at the summit, protected from the wind by stone walls, you can look forward to an exhilarating descent via the Degollada de Ucanca on a recently engineered path.

Start out at the **Parador de las Cañadas** (**O**). Follow **National Park Trail No. 4** from the turning circle next to the building. Your destination is the prominent mountain protruding out of the crater wall southeast of the *parador*.

In under 15 minutes the trail takes you to a tarred lane. Straight across is National Park Trail No. 31 (❶; your return route) but, for now, turn left to continue east along Trail No. 4. The fascinating formation of pink and yellow rocks shown on page 80 rises just in front of you. The pastel colours give this fine natural sculpture its name — **Piedras Amarillas** ('Yellow Stones'; ❷; Picnic 12). Behind them, you cross a small *cañada* (gravel plain), the **Cañada del Capricho**. Another *cañada* follows. Here Guajara — the bastion of the encircling walls — is seen at its best, rising 500m/1650ft from the crater floor. Splashes of yellow lichen, like paint daubs, decorate the higher rock faces. In spring, *taginaste rojo* — some as tall as 3m/10ft — add bold strokes of red to this canvas.

Not far beyond the turn-off left to Montaña de Majuá and the cable car (❸; Trail No. 31) you begin your ascent. The turn-off right to the Degollada de Guajara is marked with FINGERPOSTS and BOARDS for **Trail No. 31** — and also the GR131 and PR TF 86 (❹; **55min**). The clear, well-waymarked path takes you to the edge of the crater at the **Degollada de Guajara** (2373m/7785ft; ❺; **1h30min**), where the PR TF 86 and National Park Trail No. 8 head left. The views are magnificent. The tones are the most dramatic aspect of this landscape, as they flow into and across each other. *(The Shorter walk turns back here).*

View to the crater from Trail 15 on the descent to the Degollada de Ucanca

Follow **National Park Trail No. 15** southwest off the pass; it swings back to the left almost immediately. Gran Canaria seems surprisingly close from this vantage point. A little over five minutes along, at a fork marked with a METAL POLE AND A RED/WHITE 'X' (**6**), keep right on Trail No. 15 for Guajara. (The path to the left is the GR131 to Vilaflor with a connecting path to the famous 'moon landscape' — a hike described in *Landscapes of La Gomera and Southern Tenerife*.) An eroded watercourse briefly becomes your path. Metal poles help to keep you on route. The way eases out as it swings across the *retama-* and *codéso*-patched slope.

You eventually come to a fork with fingerposts showing an out-and-back path to the summit, as well as your onward path to the *parador*. Turn right here. El Teide slowly reappears until it is seen in its full magnificence when you reach the Guajara SUMMIT (**7**; **2h 30min**), marked by a trig point. There's also a rock enclosure here — a good picnic shelter on a windy winter's day, but it gets crowded. The panorama from Guajara's summit can only be matched by that from El Teide.

From the summit the descent is via the Degollada de Ucanca: return to the signposted fork and now follow the path southwest. Whereas the descent of the Guajara escarpment used to be only suitable for sure-footed hikers with a head for heights, this recently rebuilt path is clear and well waymarked, with no exposed points. As you can see in the photo above, the left side of the crater is in full view — its walls very impressive. The Llano de Ucanca is the expansive lake of gravel that lies on the edge of a dark lava flow. *Taginaste* (see page 2) flourishes amidst the rock.

The path continues through stumpy pines, heading downhill on the left side of a ridge. Just after crossing a small flat area and ascending a little, you reach the **Degollada de Ucanca** (**8**; **3h30min**). Ignore the path climbing to the left here.

Once over the pass, the cairned path (now **National Park Trail No. 31**) briefly descends to the left before swinging back to the right to make tight zigzags down the hillside. The colours in the immediate landscape are a

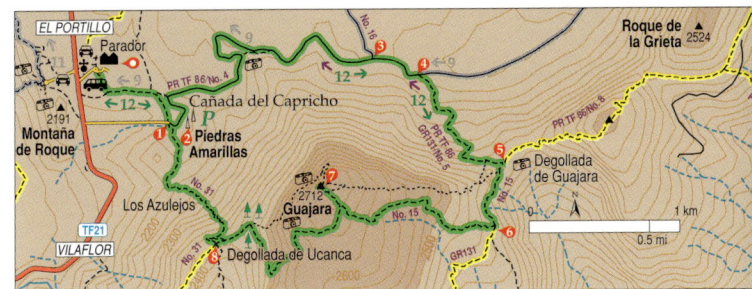

stunning mixture of green, yellow, pink, mauve and white, while over to your right are the Piedras Amarillas. Coming onto a dazzling patch of white and yellow hillside, the path veers right and soon takes you to the road, from where you follow the path directly opposite, back to the **Parador de las Cañadas** (4h30min).

Walk 13: EL PORTILLO • PIEDRA DE LOS PASTORES • GALERIA LA ZARZA • CHANAJIGA • PALO BLANCO

See also photos on pages 81, 99
Distance: 13km/8mi; 4h30min
Grade: 🔴 moderate-strenuous descent of 1450m/4750ft; some sections are very steep and *hazardous if wet*.
Equipment: walking boots, sunhat, fleece, rain-/windproof, picnic, water
Transport: 🚌 348 from Puerto to El Portillo (Timetable 5); journey time 1h. Return on 🚌 347 from Palo Blanco to La Orotava (Timetable 10); journey time 30min; *change to* 🚌 345 (Timetable 2) or 353 (Timetable 3) to Puerto; journey time 20min
Short walk: El Portillo — Choza Cruz de Fregel — El Portillo: 7km/4.3mi; 2h. 🔵 Easy descents/ascents of under 100m/330ft;

access/return on 🚌 348 as above or by 🚗 (28° 28.236'N, 16° 33.984'W); equipment as above, but trainers will suffice. Follow the main walk to ③ and return the same way.

Alternative walks
1 La Fortaleza: 13km/8mi; 4h. 🔵 Access, equipment, grade as Short walk (ascents/descents of about 200m/650ft). Do the Short walk, but visit three *miradors*. First, with La Fortaleza to your right, follow **Trail No. 1** from ② to the viewpoint at the end of the *cañada* (🅐). Retrace steps to ② or *(if it has reopened)* take the short-cut path halfway along direct to **Cruz de Fregel** (③). From there take the forestry track to the left (**Trail No. 36**), then a path, to a VIEWPOINT (🅑) at the end of the clifftops.

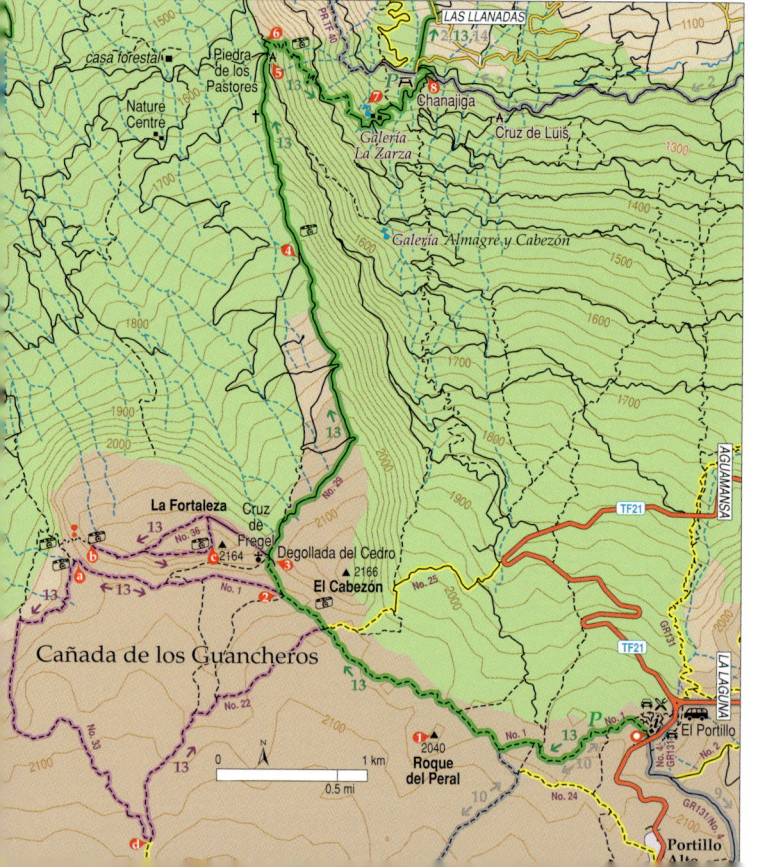

Walk 13: El Portillo to Palo Blanco and La Fortaleza   95

Again retrace steps and turn right up to the SUMMIT VIEWPOINT (**c**), then descend to the track and walk back to **El Portillo**.

2 La Fortaleza and the Cañada de los Guancheros: 13km/8mi; 4h.
● Access, equipment, grade as Alternative walk 1. Follow Alternative walk 1 to **a** then, instead of retracing your steps, head south on **National Park Trail No. 33**. This is a little tricky at first, as it crosses and rounds AA lava flows, but after about 15 minutes it becomes easy underfoot. There are a couple of short sharp ascents as the path meanders through scrub and across small *cañadas*. In a little over an hour, meeting **National Park Trail No. 22** at a T-junction (**d**), turn left. This path is a delightful, gentle downhill stroll. As it veers right towards El Cabezón there is another short sharp ascent over a lava flow, after which it soon rejoins your outbound path where you turn right back to **El Portillo**.

3 Hint: Sure-footed walkers could tackle a ● path from **a** down to the pines, then follow cairns up to the clifftops; only the first 60m/200ft of ascent are difficult.

Three scenic stretches make this walk: the volcanic world that lies at the foot of El Teide, the sunken lake of fine gravel just before you leave it, and the wooded western slopes of the Orotava Valley — now cruelly damaged by fire.

Start out on the left-hand side of the CAÑADAS VISITORS' CENTRE at **El Portillo** (**O**; daily 09.00-16.00): follow **National Park Trail No. 1**. This pretty path (Picnic 13b), shown overleaf, ends at a T-JUNCTION (**20min**), where you turn right. Soon, from a slight rise, you have a fine view to the **Roque del Peral** (**1**) on your left. Ignore turn-offs right (Trail No. 25) and left (Trail No. 22).

An exciting change takes place as you descend by the foot of **El Cabezón** to an unexpected, sunken 'lake' of fine-gravelled pumice and sand. This is **Cañada de los Guancheros** (**2**). Head west across the *cañada* near the right-hand wall (part of the *cañada* is fenced off to protect it from visitors). A few minutes across, beyond a blade of rock jutting out of the wall, *leave* Trail No. 1 and bear right on stone-lined **Trail No. 29**, climbing to a small cluster of pines that huddle in the **Degollada del Cedro**, a pass to the right of **La Fortaleza**. Here you come upon the **Cruz de Fregel** recreation area (**3**; **1h**), where three wooden crosses sit in a tiny cedar-shaded CHAPEL. But there are no seats left on which to sit and enjoy your picnic, and the *choza* has collapsed.

From here follow the forestry track downhill to the right (still Trail No. 29), ignoring Trail No. 36 climbing to the left just beyond the chapel. When last walked this trail was badly fire-damaged. A couple of minutes along, ignore a wide path on the left with a 'no entry' sign — another fire damaged path; if it's open again, use the map to follow it to the 1h50min-point at **4**.) Otherwise keep to Trail No. 29, at first on track, then on path.

You join a wide FIRE-BREAK/TRACK (**4**; **1h50min**) on the western side of a ridge and merge with another track coming from the left. Continue downhill through the frayed clearing, with some striking views over the whole Orotava Valley.

The start of the path at El Portillo on a bright winter's day

Beyond a small shrine on the left, you soon come to the **Choza Piedra de los Pastores** (the Shepherds' Rock Shelter; ❺; **2h20min**). Ignore the two tracks to the left here; go right at the T-junction just below the *choza* and then turn left immediately. The signs for 'CHANAJIGA' may be fire-damaged or missing; their metal poles remain. After about 100m/yds, on a bend to the left, take a path to the right (not signed; ❻). This was once a beautiful old woodland path zigzagging down the side of a steep ridge above the Orotava Valley. Recently it has been an unpleasant descent, strewn with burnt-out trees and dislodged rocks. After 20 minutes you cross a track and pick up the ongoing path opposite. There may be a lot of fallen trees on this stretch — either from the fires or raging storms.

Ten minutes later you leave the forest and pass **Galería La Zarza** (❼; **2h50min**; see page 44). Here the path widens out into a track, and there is likely to be forestry work going on as trees are cleared by the environmental authorities. The type of pine being removed is *not* the Canary pine, but the *Pinus insignis* — a species from the Spanish mainland introduced by General Franco in the 1950s. It is totally unfit for these regions, being a very weak pine, unable to withstand strong winds. During winter storms the trees just break up like match-sticks or toppled over because their roots are superficial. For a short time after clearance takes place the affected area looks very barren and ugly, but within a few months the indigenous vegetation regenerates.

Follow the track down towards Chanajiga. (Ignore the track joining from the right a minute along.) In 20 minutes, at a junction, head left to **Chanajiga** (❽; **3h30min**; Picnic 13a). From here use the notes for Walk 14 from ❻ (the 2h45min-point in that walk, notes on page 99) to descend to **Palo Blanco** (**4h30min**).

Walk 14: ICOD EL ALTO • LA CORONA • CHANAJIGA • PALO BLANCO

Distance: 10.8km/6.7mi; 3h45min (or 4h15min to Los Realejos)
Grade: ● strenuous, with an initial climb of 700m/2300ft and a steep descent of 600m/2000ft
Equipment: stout shoes (walking boots preferable), sunhat, fleece, rain/windproof, picnic, water
Transport: 🚌 354 from Puerto or the Realejo junction to Icod el Alto (Timetable 4); journey 35min; alight at El Dornajo (the first stop past the Mirador de El Lance). Return on 🚌 347 from Palo Blanco to La Orotava (Timetable 10); journey 30min; *change to* 🚌 345 (Timetable 2) or 353 (Timetable 3) to Puerto; journey time 20min

Shorter walk: Icod — Mirador El Asomadero — Icod: 6km/3.8mi; 2h10min. ● Strenuous ascent/descent of 500m/1650ft; access/equipment as above. Follow the main walk to ❹ (1h25min); return the same way.
Even shorter walk: La Corona — Mirador El Asomadero — La Corona: 4km/2.5mi; 1h35min. ● Moderate ascent/descent of 330m/1080ft, sometimes steep; access/equipment as above. 🚗 Motorists could park at La Corona (28° 22.679'N, 16° 36.084'W) and follow the main walk from ❷ to ❹, then return the same way.

If you've done Walk 5, you've explored the Orotava Valley from the east. On this walk, you'll get to know the west. This trek is one continuous panorama, where your views stretch far beyond the eastern escarpment. The hike ascends a ridge. And then the rural descent, equally as steep, lets you absorb the country atmosphere as you follow narrow lanes through terraced fields.

Press the button *immediately* after passing the first bus stop in Icod el Alto, which is adjacent to the Mirador de El Lance. Your stop is the *next* one. Off the bus, walk downhill to a BUS SHELTER (❍) on the opposite side of the road, where **the walk begins**. Some 15m/yds beyond the shelter, climb the lane between the houses (closed to motor traffic). You come to a road climbing steeply up from the TF342 (Calle El Lance). Keep right uphill here, quickly leaving Icod. After about **20min** of huffing and puffing, you turn off LEFT ON A TARRED LANE (❶) — the first turn-off beyond the groups of houses, about 800m/0.5mi uphill (just at the end of a high, wire fence on the right). This lane reverts to concrete, then dirt track, and soon takes you to the **Mirador La Corona** (❷; **35min**; Picnic 14), where there is also a shrine and host of antennae. The view from here is a sample of what lies further up.

Once you've absorbed it all, and worked out where each village lies, head up the ridge from the top part of the *mirador*. From here, a wide, dusty farm and forestry track leads you straight up past more antennae. Ignore all the tracks that turn off across the hillside to the right. (If you should ever be in doubt, always follow the *edge* of the ridge.)

Less than 20 minutes up, at an intersection, continue straight uphill on the middle track (an overgrown fire-break), past more antennae to the left. Around 10

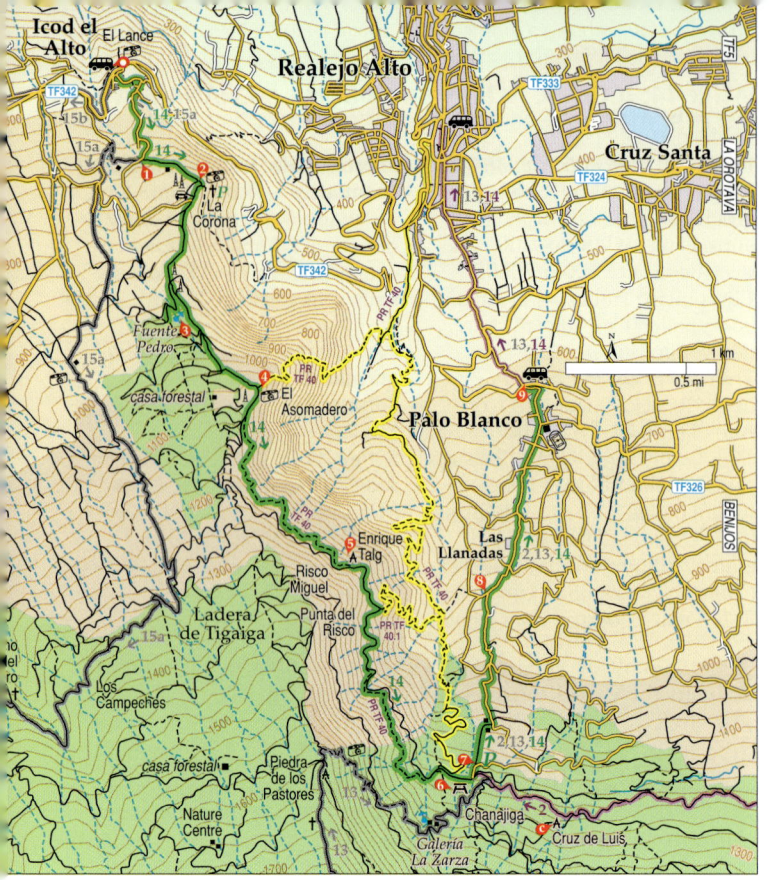

minutes from the intersection, you meet a forestry track which completes its curve and veers off to the right. Another, smaller track heads off left round the eastern face of the ridge. Again, keep straight uphill, by following the steep and skiddy middle track. (Or first turn half-right for a couple of minutes, to **Fuente Pedro** (3), a pleasant spot to take a break.) Fifteen minutes later, you join the main forestry track on a bend, then immediately leave it by forking left on another track that cuts up the edge of the escarpment. (The main track now winds up through scrub, over on your right.)

Another magnificent viewpoint, with the last antennae, the **Mirador El Asomadero** (4; 1h25min), draws you to a halt. You're overlooking farmland, a quilted patchwork of fields in the upper valley. Straight in front of you is Palo Blanco, an elongated rural settlement, clearly identified by the school. *(The Shorter walk turns back here.)*

From the *mirador* the **PR TF 40** descends to Realejo Alto, but you will follow it along the Camino del Guarda as it *climbs* to Chanajiga. Three minutes later, at an intersection, keep left uphill with the PR: there should be an information board or at least FINGERPOSTS here. For a time you are walking below the track that this walk used to follow, but you rejoin it at **Risco Miguel**, soon coming to **Choza Enrique Talg**

Right: view from the Mirador La Corona. Below: descending through spring crops at Palo Blanco

(**5**; **1h55min**). About ten minutes later, at the **Punta del Risco**, the PR TF 40.1 cuts off left to rejoin the main PR 40 route. Another FINGERPOST alerts you to where the path leaves the track again, this time running above it. Soon you're at **Chanajiga** (**6**; **2h45min**), an extensive recreation area. Walk 13 comes in here (from Piedra de los Pastores).

To make for Palo Blanco, follow the gravel road out of the picnic area for 250m/yds, to a signposted junction, where you turn left on a tarred road. Just 100m/yds downhill, on a curve, turn off left on a TRACK (**7**). A minute past two concrete farm sheds, you join a tarred country lane, where you turn left and continue downhill. On meeting a road cutting across in front of you, cross it and continue downhill on the steep tarred lane. This leads to another lane at a T-JUNCTION (**8**), where you turn right through **Las Llanadas**. Further downhill, cross straight over any junctions and keep straight down.

This very steep descent takes you through authentic rural landscapes, with hidden courtyards, flower beds, children … and dogs galore. You pass the SCHOOL on the right and continue down to the main road in **Palo Blanco** (**9**; **3h45min**), which cuts across in front of you. The BUS STOP is at the junction. Buses here in Palo Blanco are infrequent. But if you continue straight over the road, half an hour downhill, in Realejo Alto, you can pick up a bus to Puerto. (When you come to the first main street (with shops), veer right, then take the first left to the BUS STOP.)

Walk 15: TWO WALKS FROM ICOD EL ALTO

Walk 15a: Icod El Alto • El Lagar • La Guancha

See also photo on page 99
Distance: 18km/11.2mi; 7h30min
Grade: ● very strenuous and long, with a steep overall ascent of 1000m/3300ft at the start and an overall descent of 1000m/3300ft at the end. To avoid the initial climb, take a taxi to El Lagar and use the map to walk from there to Icod (ie, do the walk in reverse).
Equipment: stout shoes (walking boots preferable), sunhat, fleece, rain-/windproof, long trousers, picnic, water

Transport: 🚌 or 🚐 354 from the Puerto or the Realejo junction to Icod el Alto (Timetable 4); journey time 35min. Return on same 🚐 354 from La Guancha, or back to Icod for your car
Shorter walk: Icod el Alto — bridge — Icod el Alto: 8km/5mi; 3h50min. ● Strenuous climb/descent of 800m/2600ft; equipment and access/return as main walk. Follow the main walk to the BRIDGE just beyond the 2h30min-point at ❸ (where you join the La Guancha track) and return the same way.

On Walk a, high terraced slopes, rich in cultivation, lead you higher still — into the confines of the forest, where El Teide dominates the waves of pines. Walk b is totally different: you pursue those cultivated terraces all the way down to charming seaside villages and a lovely coastal path.

To **start Walk a**, follow Walk 14 on page 97 from the BUS STOP (⭕). At the **20min**-point (at ❶), Walk 14 heads left. Here you continue uphill to the *right*. After just 30m/yds, take the narrow path on the right down into a stream bed. At the lowest point in this path, ignore a road to the right by some houses. The path rises in a 'V', and you meet a tarred lane which you follow to the left. Cross the tarred road leading to the Mirador La Corona and head up the steep lane almost opposite. This road soon reverts to track, which ascends alongside a ravine. Rich alluvial plots step the slope on the right. Ignore all farm tracks left and right.

Twenty minutes up this track, turn RIGHT AT A T-JUNCTION (❷). Tar soon comes underfoot. Some 320m/yds from the junction, turn left up a track, towards a lone house not far above (a short-cut). Meeting the end of another tarred road, turn left uphill on its continuation — a concrete lane, which will take you almost straight uphill to the La Guancha forestry track. Montaña de Taco, a volcanic cone rising out of Buenavista's coastal plain, can be seen from here and, on clear days, La Palma is visible on the horizon.

After about 20 minutes ignore a track branching off to the right. Five minutes later, at a junction, keep right. At the next junction (which is just around the bend), the concrete lane becomes a dirt track. Take the track that heads up the left-hand side of the ravine here — not the chained-off, 'Prohibido' track, but the *next* one. Don't cross the ravine. During the next 20 minutes, keep straight uphill, ignoring side-tracks. El Teide is before you, rising above the pines, and heather cloaks the immediate slopes.

Within **2h30min** you reach the LA GUANCHA FORESTRY TRACK (❸) and turn right, soon crossing a HIGH STONE BRIDGE. *(The Shorter*

El Lagar is a very large area recreativa with camping facilities as well as pleasant barbecue areas.

walk turns back from this point.) You now follow this track, without turning off. Pass a fork off to the right and come immediately to a T-JUNCTION (**4**): go left here. The track now ascends for a while. Cross straight over an intersection at **Los Campeches** and, later, ignore another track forking off to the right. At **Lomo del Astillero** (**5**; **3h35min**), you pass a small SHRINE set back off the track. Keep an eye on the WATER PIPE beside the track from here on — the track is now appropriately named 'Pista del Tubo'.

A few minutes later, ignore the turn-off to the right; keep following the track with the water pipe. Go straight over (half-left) at the next junction and, 10 minutes later, ignore forks to the left and right (to the La Tahona recreation area). About 1km further on, ignore two tracks descending from the left. At about this point you

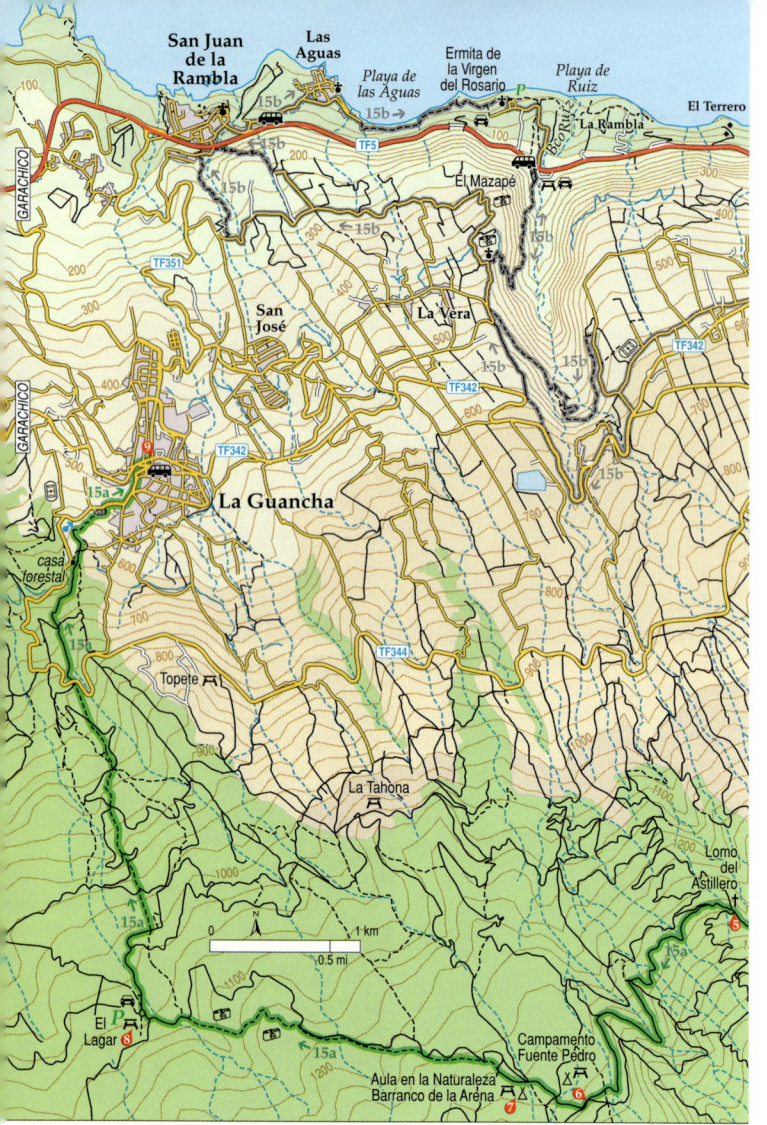

leave the Pista del Tubo (**6**), which now cuts across the hillside. A few minutes later you cross a major junction, where **Campamento Fuente Pedro** is to the right. Keep straight ahead to the **Aula en la Naturaleza Barranco de la Arena**, a campsite and picnic area (**7**; **4h40min**).

Leaving the campsite, follow the track that cuts *straight through* the picnic grounds. A couple of minutes along, you meet a track coming from the left. Follow the track to the right for 20m/yds, then take the path forking down to the left, through rocks and into the pines. In 10 minutes you rejoin the track and follow it to the left for 50m/yds. Then you rejoin your path, on the left, and head back into the woods. Ignore all the faint

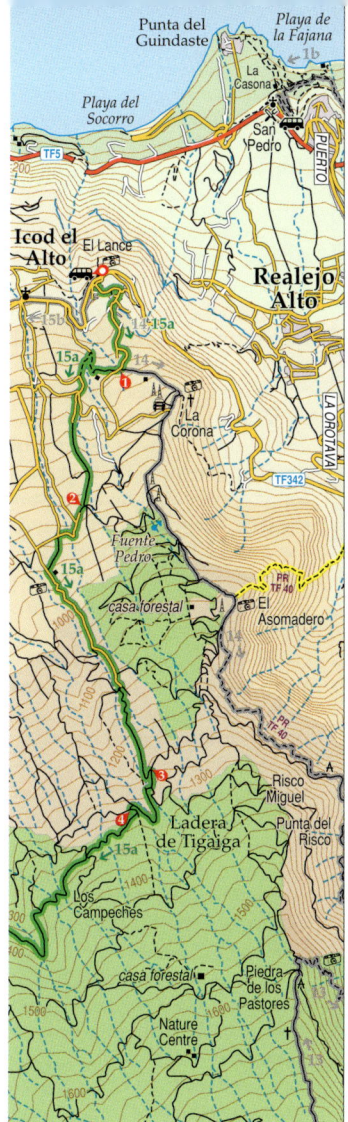

Walk 15 103

and soon another superb view beckons, as you begin to descend the left-hand side of a steep ridge. When you eventually rejoin the track, follow it down to the left and then turn right.

The **El Lagar** *zona recreativa* (**8**; **5h40min**; Picnic 15) is 100m/yds below. From here you will follow the track for a short time, but then woodcutters' paths will take you to the beautifully-sited village of La Guancha, strung along a ridge. Start down the track from El Lagar; it is signposted 'LA GUANCHA'. Around five minutes downhill, ignore the San Juan/Los Realejos turn-off (on the right). Less than five minutes later, rounding a sweeping bend, you'll see a ridge sloping down to the left. Take the path running along the top of it. It's not very clear, but just keep straight downhill. (If you miss this turn-off, you'll have another opportunity to join the path some 50m/yds downhill — see the map.) On crossing the forestry track, find the path immediately opposite. Several minutes later, you cross the track again: the path continues opposite. Cross the track again in barely two minutes and continue downhill through a particularly scenic part of the forest (the bottom of this path is slightly overgrown). You leave the woodland path again at a junction: almost exactly at the point where two tracks meet, your path re-enters the wood. Continue downhill into the bottom of a shallow gully, ignoring faint side-paths. Late in the afternoon, streams of light flicker through the dark shadows.

The path swings right and crosses over the crest. You leave the shady forest, cross the track, and enter a patch of pines. A good five

turn-offs; keep straight downhill. The track and path run parallel from time to time, and a small WATER PIPE accompanies you. Then the somewhat overgrown path rises, nestling into the slope of a ridge. Shortly you cross another low ridge: ahead of you is a superb panorama — the two humps on the horizon are La Palma. The path descends away from the pipe

The Mirador El Lance, dedicated to Prince Bentor, the last Guanche leader, who preferred to jump off a cliff rather than be taken captive by Spanish troops

minutes downhill, you cross the track again. Here veer slightly left onto an old forestry track and, 10m/yds along it, pick up the path again, dipping off to the right. The path joins an old track, and the gurgle of fast-running water from a *canal* announces the next track crossing. Go down through trees and moss.

You soon meet a tarred road (TF344): cross it and continue through pines and heather. A little way along this track, ignore the path branching off to the left. A *canal* passes under the track as it curves to the right. A minute later, go left through a small gap in the dense vegetation, following a rocky path. It takes you to another, wider path, above cultivated plots. Thick, tightly-woven moss carpets the shady corners of this path. The forest continues down past you on the left. The road is below, and the town of La Guancha is at last nearby. The sea is glistening over the pines. Enjoy these final far-reaching coastal views.

About 10 minutes down this path, you meet a junction above a lane. Descend the concrete lane, past vineyards and orchards. Streams of white dwellings come into sight, extending across the escarpment and dribbling down the ridges. Two minutes down the lane, on a sharp bend, fork right on a path (just above a large CIRCULAR WATER TANK). Keep right and come to a BASKETBALL COURT. Turn left to the tarred road. The main road (TF342) can be seen from here, in the centre of **La Guancha**. To get there, turn right down the road, go left at the T-junction and, three minutes later, descend steps on the left. Turn right on the main road. The BUS STOP is some 200m/yds ahead (**9**; **7h30min**).

Walk 15b: Mirador de El Lance • Icod El Alto • San Juan de la Rambla • Barranco de Ruiz

See also photos opposite and on pages 54-55
Distance: 12km/7.4mi; 3h30min
Grade: ● ❗ strenuous; descents of 1000m/3300ft, ascents of 500m/1650ft overall; trails are slippery when wet. The vertiginous descent to San Juan can be avoided.
Equipment: as Walk 15a
Access: 🚌 as Walk a, page 100, *but alight at the Mirador El Lance;* return on 🚌 107, 108, 325 or 363 from Barranco de Ruiz

Alternative circuit for motorists: Barranco de Ruiz — San Juan de la Rambla — Barranco de Ruiz: 8.5km/5.3mi; 2h50min. ● ❗ Grade and equipment as main walk (ascents/descents of 500m/1650ft overall). Access by 🚌 107, 108, 325 or 363 to/from Barranco de Ruiz or 🚗: park at the picnic site on the TF5 (28° 23.488'N, 16° 37.586'W). Take the signposted steps/path from the picnic site at **9** up through the lovely **Barranco de Ruiz**, climbing to the tiny CHAPEL/VIEWPOINT in **La Vera** (**3**; 50min). Follow the main walk from there back to **9**.

Start **Walk b** at the **Mirador El Lance** (**O**). Just follow the wide railed-off walkway next to the road round the Barranco de Ruiz towards Icod: the views down 600m into the *barranco* are superb! Just past the CHURCH in **Icod el Alto** (**1**; **20min**), fork right where the main road ascends to the left. Follow the road as it contours then rises above a FOOTBALL STADIUM, to an asphalted T-junction where 'BARRANCO RUIZ' is signed to the right (**40min**). (You *could* go right here for 500m to **a**, to see if the upper path across the *barranco* has reopened; it has been closed for several years and we've not been able to check it.)

Or follow the main walk by turning *left,* climbing the short way back to the main road and there turning right. After 1.4km, on the west side of the **Barranco de Ruiz,** by a WHITE-WALLED LAY-BY (**2**), turn right on a track (then path). It approaches the TN342, widens out, then emerges on a lane after another 500m. Follow this lane downhill to a tiny CHAPEL/VIEWPOINT at **La Vera** (**3**; **1h30min**), where a signposted path comes up from the **Barranco de Ruiz** PICNIC SITE on the TF5 *(Alternative circuit for motorists).*

Continue along the quiet lane as it descends in hairpins, overlooking the intensive market

Colourful San Juan de la Rambla (left and bottom; middle: chapel at La Rambla

gardening. You pass another VIEWPOINT by a defunct restaurant (**4**; **El Mazapé**), then the lane contours above the coast. Twenty minutes along, the less sure of foot could descend a lane signposted to a RESTAURANT (**5**; **1h50min**). Just past its entrance, take the tarmac lane to the left: after a short downward stretch, go straight ahead down a few wide stone steps onto a path which immediately turns right and shortly afterwards bears left to join a cobbled *camino* down to San Juan.

It's more challenging to keep to the road across a small *barranco* then around a major *barranco* with a bridge. About 100m after crossing the bridge, turn right on a dirt track beside an electricity sub-station, then follow electricity poles down towards San Juan, visible below. The well-used, stepped path descends a ridge between two *barrancos*. But it is steep and unprotected in places (the first 400m are the worst).

Approaching **San Juan de la Rambla** (**6**; **2h35min**), follow a road over the main TF5, then turn right. Arriving at the seafront (the CHURCH and plaza are to your left), turn right on Calle El Sol. At the 'no entry' sign just before the TF5/BUS STOP turn left down to the seafront promenade at **Las Aguas**. Behind the derelict SWIMMING POOL (**7**) you can follow the COASTAL PATH (a wide track, the old road before the new high-level TF5 was built). Round the headland you come to **La Rambla**. Take steps beside the 17th century CHAPEL (**8**) on your right (Picnic 15b) up to the plaza on your left and on up to the **Barranco Ruiz** PICNIC SITE and BUS STOP on the TF5 (**9**; **3h30min**).

Walk 16: LA MONTAÑETA • LAS ARENAS NEGRAS • LOS PARTIDOS DE FRANQUIS • ERJOS • LOS SILOS

See also photo on page 16
Distance: 15.5km/9.6mi; 5h
Grade: ● fairly easy but long, with an ascent of 300m/1000ft at the start and an overall descent of 1200m/4000ft — a little tough on knees. Various routes are followed, some 'official' PRs, others not (see text).
Note: Climbing Montaña Negra is no longer permitted. Please help conserve this beautiful natural site.
Equipment: walking boots, sunhat, fleece, rain-/windproof, picnic, water
Transport: 🚌 363 from Puerto to the bus station at Icod de los Vinos (Timetable 6); journey time 45min; then *change to* 🚌 360 and ask for 'Ermita de San Francisco', at the top end of La Montañeta village (Timetable 8); journey time 35min. Return on 🚌 363 from Los Silos to Puerto (Timetable 6); journey time 1h10min.

Shorter walks
1 La Montañeta — Montaña Negra — La Montañeta:
8.5km/5.3mi; 2h30min. ● Fairly easy ascent/descent of 300m/1000ft; access as above or by 🚗 (28° 20.133'N, 16° 45.551'W); return on the same buses; equipment as above, but stout shoes will suffice. Follow the main walk to and along the **Canal Vergara** (❸), then return on the **PR TF 43** (❶).
2 La Montañeta — Las Arenas Negras — Los Partidos de Franquis — Restaurante Fleytas:
10.5km/6.5mi; 3h. ● Fairly easy, with an ascent of 300m/1000ft at the start; access/equipment as above, but stout shoes will suffice. Or 🚗 to Restaurante Fleytas (28° 19.066'N, 16° 43.312'W), then 🚌 360 to the start. Return on 🚌 325 from Restaurante Fleytas to Puerto (Timetable 16); journey time 1h15min. Or return on 🚌

The pines at Las Arenas Negras almost look fluorescent.

460 to Icod de los Vinos (Timetable 7); journey time 40min; *change to* 🚐 363 from Icod to Puerto (Timetable 6); journey time 45min. Follow the walk up to the ROUNDABOUT at ❻ (2h40min), where the main walk turns right. Turn *left* to **Restaurante Fleytas** (🅒) on the TF82, 15min away.

3 San José de los Llanos — Montaña Negra — Canal Vergara — Las Arenas Negras — La Montañeta: 7.6km/4.7mi; 1h45min. ● Fairly easy, with an ascent of 250m/820ft and descent of 400m/1300ft; access/return and equipment as main walk, but stout shoes will suffice. Rather than alight from the bus at La Montañeta, stay on to **San José de los Llanos**. The bus drops you off in front of the CHURCH (🅓), by a large trail map for the PR TF 43. Take the lane directly opposite the church, signposted to 'CHINYERO'. The lane (**PR TF 43.1**) climbs briefly before signs guide you right, then left at junctions. On the edge of the village, 50m from the final T-junction, the path heads off into the pines. It's a steady gradual climb through the forest of about 40 minutes on a path covered with pine needles and lined with stones on both sides. You cross a couple of minor tracks and pass a SHRINE. The crunch of volcanic ash underfoot signals you are near the top at **Montaña Negra**. The path zigzags the last couple of minutes up to the **Pista Canal de Vergara** (❸) beside the **Canal Vergara**. Turn left and follow the track beside the *canal* in the opposite direction to the main walk, *leaving* the PR for the time being. Ten-15 minutes along, beyond a BARRIER, the **PR TF 43** crosses the track. Turn left downhill here. Towards the end of this section the track followed in the main walk ascent runs parallel with the path. Just a few yards before the PR path joins the track, continue down the natural gully, with the track up to your right. Almost immediately you are in **Las Arenas Negras** PICNIC SITE (❶). From here either follow the main walk ascent track in reverse or descend the PR TF 43 signed to 'LA MONTAÑETA'.

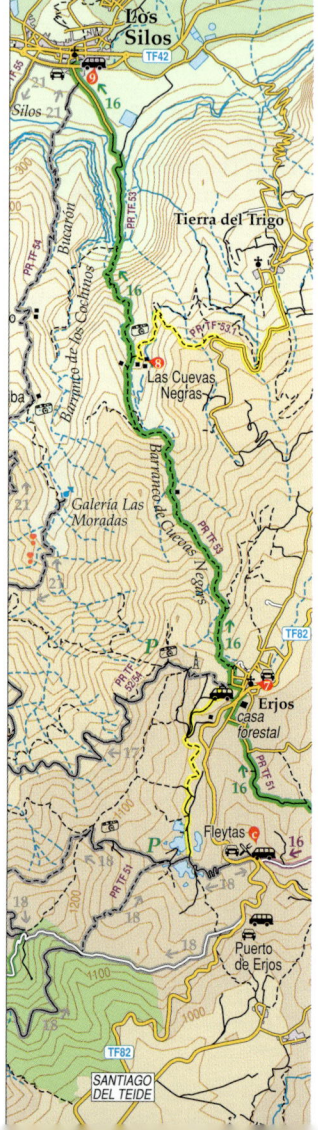

Walk 16: From La Montañeta to Los Silos   109

This is one of my favourite hikes, packed with spectacular scenery. The black mound of Las Arenas Negras and its surrounding sands provides us with the volcanic touch. Out of the sands, we pass through wild, open country, high above a plain. A brief transition to lush grassy slopes follows, as we descend. Later, crossing a plain, we are enveloped in a forest of *escobón*. And on the final leg, down a hidden valley, an old path leads us through a great tangle of vegetation, first through laurel forest and then down a defile with a wealth of exotic plant life.

The walk starts at **La Montañeta** (**○**), on the path signed 'PR TF 43', just uphill from the bus stop and across the road from a chapel, the **Ermita San Francisco**. In just one minute, *ignore* the PR TF 43 turning left and crossing the road on a footbridge. (Of course there is no reason why you shouldn't follow this newer, well-waymarked trail up to the Canal Vergara if you prefer — Shorter walk 1 descends it.) Your route, lesser used and *not* officially waymarked, goes straight ahead up the hill. In five minutes you meet an old track and turn left uphill. Cross the Los Llanos road (TF373) and, shortly after, the forestry track to Las Arenas Negras. Ignore two turn-offs left three minutes later. Meeting a THREE-WAY JUNCTION (**20min**), go straight ahead on the main forestry track. Having ignored a faint fork off to the right and another to the left, you reach **Las Arenas Negras** (**❶**; **40min**; Picnic 16).

Continue up the track. Immediately upon entering the picnic area and children's playground, turn left alongside the low stone wall. Just before a stone building with a tiled roof, TURN RIGHT (**❷**) up the forestry track. Just over 20 minutes up, keep an eye out for TWO SMALL CONCRETE BUILDINGS

in the trees on your right. They are perched on one of the island's longest and most important watercourses, the **Canal Vergara** (**1h05min**). **Galería Vergara Alta**, and the *canal* it feeds, are responsible for a large supply of water conveyed to the southern side of the island; the system has been operating since the early 1950s. This gallery goes back some 3.5 kilometres (over two miles) into the mountainside, and they're still excavating!

Fork right on the track just below the *canal*, the **Pista Canal de Vergara** (❸) — walking atop the watercourse is not allowed (although the 'Prohibido' signs have disappeared). Head back towards the volcanic fields of black sand, into the alluring confines of Montaña Negra. This stark enclosed landscape comes ablaze as the sand shimmers and the encircling pines flicker under the bright sun.

Before long, you find the trees thinning out and the sands opening up ahead. You pass the PR TF 43 heading down to the right (🅐). *(For Shorter walk 1, take this path and, when you get back to the picnic grounds, continue down the PR TF 43 all the way to La Montañeta.)* Clusters of sharp grey rock attract your attention with their patchy coating of thick rusty-orange lichen. **Montaña Negra** is now beside you on the right. Pines, planted out symmetrically in a hollow immediately ahead, catch the eye. Continuing to the left, you see a long rough tail of crusted lava heading seaward. Soon the PR TF 43.1 heads off right to San José de los Llanos (🅑; **1h35min**). *(Shorter walk 3 ascends this trail.)*

Heading on, you briefly re-enter the pines, then exit through a control barrier. Soon a magnificent viewpoint greets you. On a clear day, La Gomera can be seen clearly — even its villages! To the right lie the twin humps of La Palma. Los Llanos betrays its secluded location on the far right. Some 30 minutes from Montaña Negra, at a junction of four tracks, turn right — either on the track or on the PR TF 43

Walk 16: From La Montañeta to Los Silos 111

short-cut. About 10 minutes down ignore a track to the right; make your way across a plain forested in *escobón* — a beautiful sight in March when the trees are in bloom. At the next two junctions (the first being **Corral Nueva** (**4**), where the PR TF 51 goes right to San José de los Llanos), keep straight on.

The hamlet of **Los Partidos de Franquis** (**5**) is barely noticeable — it's all but deserted — save for a lovely small countryside hotel, the Caserío Los Partidos. As you leave the basin, more signs of cultivation appear. Beyond the hamlet, you meet the ROAD TO SAN JOSÉ DE LOS LLANOS at a roundabout (**6**; **2h40min**). Cross straight over and follow the **PR TF 51** to Erjos. *(But for Shorter walk 2, follow the road to the left for 170m/yds, then turn right to Restaurante Fleytas on the TF82.)*

Coming into **Erjos**, keep right, then go left just before the SCHOOL. At the junction, turn right. Cross the TF82 and head down to the CHURCH (**7**; **3h 10min**). Turn sharp left here and, just over the crest, turn right for 'LOS SILOS'. You now follow the **PR TF 53** all the way to your destination. When the street ends, continue on a path down into the *barranco*. Keep straight on past the houses, several of which belong to those enjoying an 'alternative lifestyle'. The *barranco* floor is overgrown, with neglected plots. Soon you disappear into the woods. Sagging stone walls with moss-covered rocks flank the path. Fifty minutes from Erjos you pass a beautiful OLD DWELLING in an overgrown garden behind stone walls (**4h**).

Little houses on the *barranco* wall over to the right are the first signs of the isolated hamlet of **Las Cuevas Negras** (**8**). Most of them are buried in hillside vegetation. Crossing the *barranco,* you encounter a few more derelict buildings and pass a path ascending to the houses. This is a delightful spot. The plains of Los Silos appear through the V in the valley, which narrows to a defile of high jagged walls. The path steepens, and you pass below an impressive rockface. Stepping down out of the *barranco,* you come to luxuriant garden plots, orchards, and banana groves. A rough concrete lane takes you out of the valley. Seven minutes down the lane, you cross the *barranco* at a ford. Some 100m/yds further on, turn left on a path that crosses the *barranco* via a small wooden bridge. Another bridge follows, and you then turn right down a lane to the valley floor. The BUS STOP (**9**) in **Los Silos** is at the junction of the bypass road and Calle Susana, just south of the CHURCH PLAZA (**5h**).

Before catching the bus, do visit the church plaza in Los Silos

Walk 17: ERJOS • LAS LAGUNETAS • EL PALMAR

See also photo pages 32-33
Distance: 10.5km/6.5mi; 3h25min
Grade: ● fairly easy descent of 500m/1650ft on tracks; PR TF 52 and 52.1
Equipment: stout shoes, sunhat, fleece, windproof, water, picnic
Transport: 🚐 325 from Puerto to Erjos (Timetable 16); journey time 1h15min. Return on 🚐 366 from El Palmar to Buenavista (Timetable 11); journey time 15min; *change to* 🚐 363 for Puerto (Timetable 6); journey time 50min.

Alternative walks
1 Erjos — Los Lavaderos — Erjos: 13km/8mi; 4h10min. ●
Moderate, but with a tiring ascent of 300m/1000ft at the end. Equipment as above, but hiking boots recommended. Access/return by 🚐 325 (as above) or 🚗 to/from Erjos (28° 19.654'N, 16° 48.299'W). You could also return on 🚐 460 to Icod de los Vinos, then *change to* 🚐 363 for Puerto (as Walk 16, page 107). Follow the main walk to the *second* **Las Moradas** TURN-OFF at ❹ (1h40min). Keep right here, and continue down the track for a further 35 minutes. Watch for an abandoned concrete building above the track and, two minutes beyond it, turn right uphill on a path (❶; the **PR TF 54**), climbing the bed of a *barranco*. Three minutes up, turn left on another path cutting around the hillside (still the PR TF 54). Follow this path up to the ERJOS/EL PALMAR FORESTRY TRACK at ❷, 35 minutes uphill. Now retrace your outgoing route back to **Erjos**, 1h25min away.

2 Erjos — Los Lavaderos — Los Silos: 12.2km/7.6mi; 4h. ● Fairly easy, but the descent of 900m/3000ft is a little tough on the knees. Equipment and access as main walk; return as Walk 21 (page 126). Follow the main walk to the *second* **Las Moradas** TURN-OFF at ❹ (1h40min), then pick up **Walk 21** at its 2h55min-point (at ❺) and follow it to the end.

This is a pleasant, easy stroll, through a relic of the Tertiary period — the great laurel forest which covered southern Europe and North Africa some 15 million years ago. Today these flora are virtually extinct, but the Canarian archipelago harbours a few of the remaining sanctuaries. This evergreen forest is the result of climatic conditions brought about by the trade winds. At least ten species of laurel flourish here; the forest is also a refuge for ferns, fungi and lichen.

The bus ride itself brightens your day: the first thing to hit you will be the splendour of the colours — bright red poinsettias, blue morning glory, white, pink and red

Walking to El Palmar on the Camino las Huertas, you pass to the east of the Montañeta del Palmar. But since the quarrying is on its west *side (opposite the road to Teno Alto), you may be unaware of this intriguing landscape.*

Walk 17: From Erjos to El Palmar

oleander, and the ever-present bougainvillea, with its rich hues of scarlet, orange and purple. Canary date palms give the road a touch of elegance. You'll pass through picturesque San Juan de la Rambla and then come into the pleasant sprawling town of Icod de los Vinos (known for the dragon tree shown on page 29). The ongoing route to Erjos climbs 800m/2600ft and affords some of the most splendid panoramas on the island, from intensively tilled rich pockets of volcanic soil to wild, untamed greenery, where Erjos is just a meek splash of white.

You'll be dropped off just past the CHURCH (O) in **Erjos**. **Start out** by taking the steps alongside the church (fingerpost 'LAS PORTELAS'), then follow the road opposite the church entrance. Just over the crest, the road veers sharp right: keep straight ahead downhill on a path beside a house. The path turns right and goes downhill to cross a ravine. At another fingerpost ('**PR 52** PORTELAS'), head right to climb the hillside on another path, making for a prominent RED AND WHITE COMMUNICATIONS MAST (❶). Around 10 minutes up, you're out on the forestry track, which you will follow all the way to the El Palmar Valley, over two hours away. There are two springs en route.

A couple of minutes along the track you're overlooking a cauldron of valleys (Picnic 17). Beyond the FIRST SPRING, you pass the PR TF 54 off right to Las Moradas (❷). Beyond the SECOND SPRING (❸), you come into another, equally impressive basin where a track off right goes to Las Moradas (❹; **1h40min**). *(If you're doing either of the Alternative walks, turn right here despite the wrong way 'X'; this track is also used in Walk 21.)*

Within the next 30 minutes you pass the PR TF 52.1 (❺) descending to the right, where Walk 21 joins, before heading towards Erjos. (El Palmar can also be reached via this track, as in Shorter walk 21.) Continue left on the PR TF 52 for 'LAS PORTELAS'. Not far along, you come into the treeless **El Palmar Valley** (**2h20min**): the entire basin is terraced, from top to bottom, right to left. El Palmar lies almost immediately below and, much further down on the plain, Buenavista sits surrounded by banana palms.

Some 25 minutes after coming into the valley, leave the track (just beyond a bend). The turn-off is signposted '**PR TF 52.2** EL PALMAR' (❻; **2h45min**). Descend the path to the right, then keep left uphill at a fork. The path threads its way through abandoned and overgrown plots. Large unruly fig trees abound and, in spring, mauve and purple *Senecio* (see page 129)

bloom along the route. Just over 10 minutes downhill, you come into the picturesque village of **Las Lagunetas** (❼), passing some houses.

On reaching a crossroads, turn right. You now follow '**PR TF 56** EL PALMAR POR LAS HUERTAS' (❽). This incredibly bucolic lane, edged with a profusion of colourful blooms, brings you into **El Palmar** (**3h25min**). Turn left on the main road (TF436): the BUS STOP (❾) is 100m/yds away. Or, if you're still full of energy, use the map on page 127 to follow the old stone-paved track (tarred at the outset) to Buenavista, 40 minutes away.

If you do go into Buenavista, make time to go to the coast. This lovely viewpoint is just west of where Short walk 20 ends.

Walk 18: RESTAURANTE FLEYTAS • MONTAÑA JALA • LOS BOLICOS • DEGOLLADA DE LA MESA • RESTAURANTE FLEYTAS

Distance: 12.2km/7.6mi; 4h05min
Grade: ● moderate, with overall ascents/descents of 550m/1800ft. The ascent to Pico Verde requires a little scrambling; some people will find it vertiginous (❗). The weather can be very changeable; you can be engulfed in cloud within minutes.
Equipment: hiking boots, sunhat, suncream, rain-/windproof, fleece, picnic, water
Transport: 🚌 325 from Puerto to/from Restaurante Fleytas, above Erjos (Timetable 16; journey time 1h15min), or by 🚗 (28° 19.066'N, 16° 43.312'W). Alternative return buses are 460 and 360 (the latter via La Montañeta).

Short walk: Restaurante Fleytas — Los Bolicos — Restaurante Fleytas: 8.2km/5.1mi; 2h25min.
● Quite easy, with overall ascents/descents of about 300m/1000ft; equipment and access as main walk. Follow the main walk, but omit the two ascents to the peaks.

Alternative walks
1 Puerto de Erjos — Montaña Jala — La Tabaiba — Teno Alto — Buenavista: 18km/11.2mi; 6h.
● *Only suitable for experienced, adventurous hikers,* on account of the very steep (700m/2300ft) and vertiginous descent from Teno Alto; otherwise, see Alternative walks 2 and 3. Equipment/access as main walk (🚌 325); return from Buenavista on 🚌 363 to Puerto (Timetable 6); journey time 1h20min. Alight from the bus at **Puerto de Erjos** (**a**), at the junction with the road to **Montaña Jala**. Follow the road to the SUMMIT (**5**; 35min). Descend the same way for 10min, then fork left on a track to **4** (ignore the track striking off right immediately into the turn-off). Within the next 10 minutes, just past a track forking right, bear left on a path. A couple of minutes later, at a junction of paths (**b**; **Cruce de Jala**), descend to the right. At the fork, both branches lead down to the derelict hamlet of **Los Bolicos** (**7**; 1h05min). Leave the hamlet on the track to the left of it; it soon becomes a path (**PR TF 51**). Within five minutes, fork left to a viewpoint. Then return to the junction and go left. Remain on this ridge (**Cumbre de Masca**, then **Cumbre del Carrizal**), keeping straight ahead at the ONLY JUNCTION (**c**; *where Alternative walk 3 goes left on the PR TF 59)*, until you cross the TF436 at the pass of **La Tabaiba** (**d**; **Mirador de Baracán**; 2h10min). Here pick up **Walk 19** (page 120), to continue up the *cumbre* and descend to Buenavista.

2 Puerto de Erjos — Montaña Jala — La Tabaiba — Teno Alto — La Montañeta: 16km/10mi; 5h50min. ● Moderate; overall ascent 350m, descent 1100m; equipment as main walk; access as Alternative walk 18-1. Follow Alternative walk 18-1 to **Teno Alto**, then switch to Alternative walk 19 to go from there to **La Montañeta del Palmar** along the **PR TF 57** (1h15min). Return from La Montañeta on 🚌 366 to Buenavista (Timetable 11); journey time 15min, then *change to* 🚌 363 for Puerto (Timetable 6); journey time 1h20min.

3 Puerto de Erjos — Montaña Jala — El Turrón: 8.8m/5.5mi; 2h30min. ● Easy-moderate; overall ascent 250m, descent 850m; equipment and access as

116 Landscapes of Tenerife

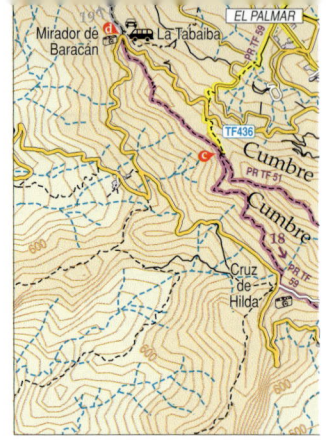

Alternative walk 1. This one calls for a few changes of bus! Follow Alternative walk 1 along the ridge then, referring to the map, turn left downhill on the **Cumbre del Carrizal** with the **PR TF 59** at C (the 'only junction'). You join the TF436 at the **Cruz de Hilda** (*mirador,* BAR/RESTAURANT). From here follow the PR TF 59 towards 'MASCA', cutting a deep bend off the road. When you meet the road again at a place called **Es Turrón**, there is a BUS STOP opposite, beside another BAR/RESTAURANT. From here take 🚐 355 to Santiago del Teide (Timetable 11, departs Es Turrón at about 12.15, 16.00, 18.10), where you change to 🚐 460 to Icod and then change again to 🚐 363 to Puerto. Phew!

T he few ponds encountered (Tenerife's 'Lake District'!) set this walk apart from the others. Beyond them, after enjoying a stupendous view from the highest point in the western corner of the island, we follow a jungle-like trail, dripping with moss, before scrambling up to a lesser peak, even more exhilarating than the first.

Start out at **Restaurante Fleytas**, the BUS STOP (O) above Erjos. Walk back down the road towards Erjos for 100m/yds, then fork left on a track, down to the valley floor. Here you'll see several lovely ponds — if there has been adequate rainfall! Montaña Jala — your destination — is the highest point just behind the hill in the foreground. Down by the ponds, you come to a T-JUNCTION (❶). Turn right here and, 70m/yds further on, take the track forking off to the left. It will take you up to the ridge over on the right.

Luxuriant vegetation greets you. The whole basin (Picnic 18a) is wild and unkempt, and many of the terraced plots are overgrown. Just past two ponds, you pass through a STAGGERED JUNCTION: follow the main track as it curves

Pond at Erjos

to the right. Walk *past* the first left (the signposted PR TF 51, your return route), then take the *second* track to the left, at first walking below the PR trail. As your track ascends, ignore any farm tracks forking off to the left or right.

About 10 minutes up from the basin there may be a chain across the track; if so, just walk past it. Keep straight uphill; in five minutes you're on the crest of the ridge, with a magnificent view of El Teide and a good outlook over the ponds below. A minute later, at a junction of paths to the left, keep right (**30min**; CAIRN), rounding the hillside and entering the woods. Cool, fresh, and laden with moss, your path provides a pleasant interlude on hot days. Ignore all descending paths.

A little over 10 minutes along, at a JUNCTION (**❷**), ascend to the left on another path. *(But for the Short walk, continue straight ahead round the hillside and pick up the notes again from the 1h30min-point.)* Immediately over a small crest, veer right to cross a small *barranco*, then ignore a path to the left. Several minutes later, meet a forestry track (CAIRN) and turn left uphill (❸; NOTE THE LAY-BY here — also with a CAIRN — to relocate the path on your return).

Some 450m/yds further on, as the TRACK BENDS TO THE RIGHT (❹), rise up a small earthen bank on the left (opposite a small brown metal gate), to join the forestry road to the summit. Follow the road to the right for just over 10 minutes, up to the antennae and fire-watch tower on **Montaña Jala** (❺; **1h10min**). What a view! You look straight down on the cataclysm of ravines that carve up this western massif. To the south, hundreds of greenhouses sparkle under the sun. Santiago del Teide is the small settlement in the shallow valley below on the left.

Moving on, you return to the laurel forest ... the best of which is still to come. Retrace your steps back down the road and then the track. By the LAY-BY (❸), pick up your ascending path and return to the JUNCTION (❷; **1h30min**). *(The Short walk rejoins here.)* Turn left and, a minute along, at a fork, head right downhill, to a beautiful spot, where the trees and rocks are cloaked in thick moss and a SPRING (❻) sits below a wall of basalt.

Back at the fork, turn right, to ascend to the top of the ridge. Stay to the right of the 'clearing'. Ignore the faint fork off to the left here; keep round the edge of the valley on the sometimes-overgrown path. (If this path becomes impassable, you will have to retrace your steps and use the map to follow the track to Los Bolicos.) Ten minutes from the spring you meet a wider path and turn left. At the intersection a couple of minutes uphill, turn right downhill (CAIRN). Ten minutes later, having kept right at a Y-fork, you come into the derelict hamlet of **Los Bolicos** (❼; **2h30min**), sheltering in a hollow on the ridge. This is a good place to see the bright red and yellow parasitic plant, *Cytinus hypocistis*, which resembles a fungus.

From here you ascend to the right of Montaña Jala, to the pointed rocky peak on your left. Walk back up to the path and track on the right (signposted 'PUERTO DE ERJOS'; **PR TF 51**) and climb the hillside (the path and track rejoin). The path veers left and rounds a narrow valley. Ignore a turn-off to the left. Twenty minutes up, you're at the **Degollada de la Mesa** (❽; **2h55min**), with the peak just to the right. *(If you're doing the Short walk, keep straight on over this pass; see last paragraph.)* Poke around in the bushes to find the path to the peak; it *does* exist and remains on the crest all the way up, waymarked with the odd green dot. A good 10 minutes gets you to the top, the summit of **Pico Verde** (❾), surrounded by sheer drops and enjoying a superb view into the valley of Masca below.

Back at the pass, descend a slope lightly wooded in pines. When you reach the forestry track, follow it for a little over 20 minutes, up to the Montaña Jala road. Cross straight over, still on the PR TF 51, an old donkey trail. Some 10 minutes down, you meet your outgoing path at the STAGGERED JUNCTION (❷) and turn right, back up to the BUS STOP at **Restaurante Fleytas** (**4h05min**).

Walk 19: LA TABAIBA • TENO ALTO • BUENAVISTA

See also photos on pages 14-15, 32-33 and 125
Distance: 10.5km/6.5mi; 3h30min
Grade: ● ❗ moderate-strenuous, with an ascent of 200m/650ft and a steep, rocky descent of 600m/1970ft. You must be sure-footed and have a head for heights (danger of vertigo); *the descent is only recommended for very experienced hikers* (otherwise, do the Alternative walk below or do the main walk in reverse ●: climbing is always less difficult than descending). *The walk is only suitable in fine weather.* PR TF 51, then PR TF 58
Equipment: hiking boots, warm fleece, sunhat, rain-/windproof, suncream, picnic, water
Transport: 🚌 363 from Puerto to Buenavista (Timetable 6); journey time 1h20min; *change to* 🚌 355 to the pass of La Tabaiba/Mirador de Baracán (Santiago bus, Timetable 11) — or take a taxi (5km). It's the highest point on the road to Masca, by the KM12 signpost, and there is a large parking bay. Return on 🚌 363 from Buenavista to Puerto (Timetable 6); journey time 1h20min

Alternative walk: La Tabaiba — Teno Alto — La Montañeta: 8.5km/5.3mi; 2h40min. ● Moderate; equipment and access as above; return on 🚌 366 to Buenavista (Timetable 11); journey time 15min; *change to* 🚌 363 to Puerto (as above). Follow the main walk (PR TF 51) to **Teno Alto**, then take the **PR TF 57** to **La Montañeta del Palmar** (the first part of Walk 20, but in reverse). *Note:* the initial five-minute descent back into the El Palmar Valley is very steep and slippery; use the road if this looks too difficult.

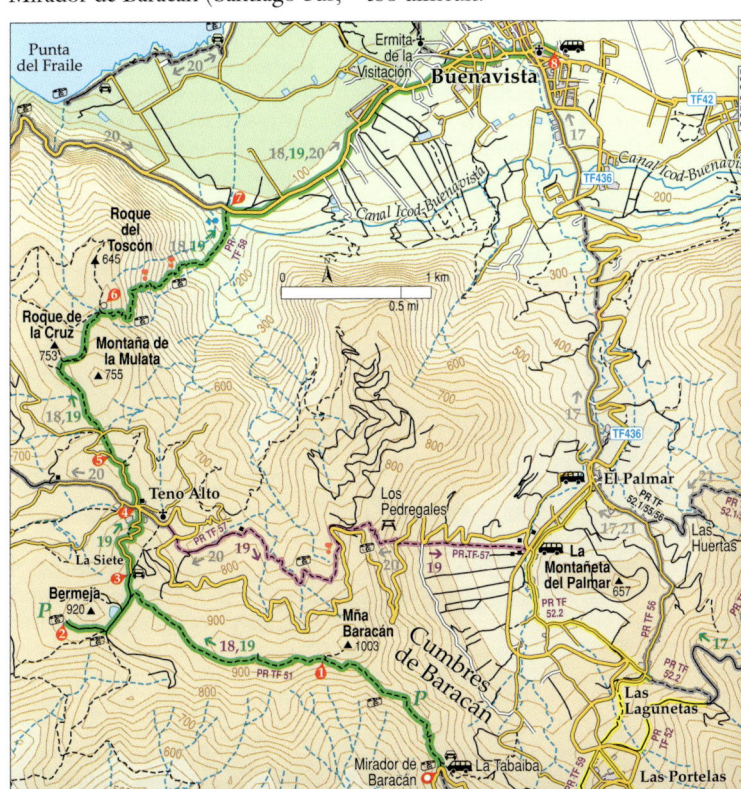

120 Landscapes of Tenerife (Cañadas • Orotava • Teno • Anaga)

Spectacular, exhilarating and, in places, hair-raising ... but if you are sure-footed and not affected by vertigo, I highly recommend this hike. It dissects the hills of Teno: rocky ridges offering stunning views, plunging gullies, goatherds and lush meadows. The final descent has to be one of the most impressive in the archipelago!

Alight from the bus or taxi at the pass of **La Tabaiba/Mirador de Baracán** (**○**), at the KM12 road marker. **Start out** by following the well signposted and waymarked trail (**PR TF 51**) off the parking bay, heading north for 'PUNTA DE TENO' and 'TENO ALTO'. There is a superb view over the verdant cultivation in the El Palmar Valley on the right; to the left, you look across sheer plunging ravines. Your route heads up the **Cumbres de Baracán** (Picnic 19a), towards Montaña Baracán, the highest point; later, it will swing across to the left, to the heights of Teno. The slopes are a tapestry of wild flowers in spring, and goat bells tinkle in the valleys below. Los Carrizales is the small village far below to the left.

You pass a path ascending to **Montaña Baracán** (**❶**; **30min**). As the view from its summit has little more to offer, continue to the left. On reaching the top of the ridge, you look straight out over a dissected tableland. Teno Alto is the tight cluster of houses sheltering at the foot of a hill below you. Other scattered dwellings sprinkle the tops of ridges. The banana plantations of Buenavista appear through the walls of a *barranco* and, behind you, the massive shoulders of El Teide rise spectacularly.

Crossing over the ridge, you head into scrub, stride across grassy slopes, and then dip into a beautiful wood of heather. Below the wood you come to the edge of La Siete. Before entering the hamlet, turn left on a track — to a wide hillside 'balcony' with the stupendous view shown below: a landscape of razor-sharp ridges. A little further on, turn right on a path — to an even better VIEW-POINT (**❷**), overlooking a tilting plateau of grassland with the scattered homesteads of a few

Walk 19: La Tabaiba • Teno Alto • Buenavista 121

goatherds. The only sound is the tinkling of goats' bells — and yappy herders' dogs. This is my favourite part of Teno; I could sit here forever ... when the wind isn't blowing (Picnic 19b).

Onward bound, head back down the track to **La Siete** (❸), from where you follow a lane in a short winding descent to **Teno Alto** (❹; **1h25min**). *(Those doing the Alternative walk should now use the map on page 119 to continue to La Montañeta: follow Walk 20, but in reverse.)* The main walk leaves Teno on the road ascending to the left of Bar Los Bailaderos (**PR TF 58**, signposted 'BUENAVISTA'). The Buenavista flats reappear, down through a deep ravine. A few minutes along, just after a track forks off to the right, turn right downhill on a WIDE DIRT PATH (❺). This steep descent brings you back to the road at a PASS where the road bends left and a track forks off it to the right. Cross the track and ascend the ridge ahead (still the PR TF 58). Your path soon swings right, to pass between two hills: the prominent pointed one on the left is **Roque de la Cruz** (**1h40min**).

There may be a fingerpost here for 'BUENAVISTA'). Your path is the lower one to the right, which descends into the lush valley below. A patch of eroded hillside opposite catches the eye, with its breathtaking array of soft volcanic pinks, mauves, creams, and browns. Remains of a cobbled path come underfoot. You drop into a shallow V in the top of the crest and pass a circular area surrounded by a low stone wall — an ancient GUANCHE SITE (❻; **1h45min**). Here the path appears to disappear off the cliffs ahead ... and almost does!

Before the descent, enjoy the brilliant view over Buenavista and along the coast. Climbing a short way out of the dip, you find a gate, beyond which the descent path clings to a narrow ledge. Chiselled out of the sheer rock face and vertiginous from the outset, it bears the traces of former paving. As you zigzag down, be sure to *stop* to admire the views — and the surprising amount of plant life, including patches of rusty-red and lime-yellow lichen, *tabaiba, candelabra,* and *Aeoniums.* Closer to the *barranco* floor, the vegetation is head-high and jungle-thick. An hour down the cliff path, you're in the bed of a dry *barranco*. Swinging in and out of the *barranco,* you clamber over rocks and boulders.

Reaching a track, follow it to the TF445 (❼; **2h45min**). Follow the road to the right, into **Buenavista**. Keep straight ahead past the Plaza San Sebastián (on your right) to the BUS STATION (❽; on your left; **3h30min**). If you have time to look around the village, why not walk down to the seaside chapel and coastal path (see Short walk 20 overleaf).

Viewpoint above La Siete (Picnic 19b)

Walk 20: LA MONTAÑETA (EL PALMAR) • TENO ALTO • TENO BAJO • (FARO DE TENO) • BUENAVISTA

See also photos on pages 14-15, 32-33 and 114
Distance: 16km/9.9mi; 5h30min (add 1h for a detour to the lighthouse or take 🚐 369 to the point and back to Buenavista, saving 3h walking; see the foot of page 161)
Grade: ●! strenuous, with a total climb of 400m/1300ft and descent of 800m/2600ft. There is the additional hazard of loose stones on the final descent. Possibility of vertigo on two short-cut paths. PRTF 57, then PR TF 51
Equipment: walking boots, sunhat, fleece, rain-/windproof, picnic, plenty of water, swimwear; a torch is *essential* for the road tunnel, or take the bus (as above) from ❽
Transport: 🚐 363 from Puerto to Buenavista (Timetable 6); journey time 1h20min; *change to* 🚐 366 to El Palmar (Timetable 11); journey time 15min; ask for 'el camino para Teno Alto'. Or take a taxi for this trip of 5km. Return on 🚐 363 from Buenavista to Puerto (Timetable 6; as above)
Short walk: Buenavista coastal path: 8km/5mi; 2h10. ● Easy; equipment as above, but stout shoes will suffice. Access/return with 🚐 363 to Buenavista (Timetable 6); journey time 1h20min. Or by 🚗: Travelling by car, there are several parking places (all shown on the map) to shorten the walk. Using the map, start from Plaza San Sebastián (ⓐ) west of the BUS STATION. Head north on the street opposite the **San Sebastián** CHAPEL. Walk to the left of the main CHURCH, turn left at a T-junction, then fork left 100m/yds short of the CEMETERY entrance. Coming down to a seaside CHAPEL (ⓑ; Picnic 20b) at the **Mirador Barqueros**, follow the lovely coastal path north of the GOLF COURSE to **Playa de las Arenas** (ⓒ). From the end of the beach, cross the bridge shown on pages 14-15 and continue to **Playa del Fraile** (ⓓ), where the path ends. Retrace steps past the Mirador Barqueros and after 200m/yds, at a fingerpost, turn right up an old trail signed 'CENTRO HISTORICO' and 'ERMITA DE LA VISITACION'. Beyond the pretty *ermita* (ⓔ), walk on to the TF445 and turn left, back to Plaza San Sebastián.

Walk 20: From La Montañeta del Palmar to Buenavista

The high, hidden, segmented valleys of the Teno are a must for those with stamina. This isolated severe landscape has a stark beauty, with soft colours emanating from the earth itself. Solitude and peace immediately come to mind. The hardships that these few inhabitants have chosen to face leave one admiring, perhaps even envying, their fortitude.

The walk begins just by the road to Teno Alto: take the **PR TF 57** (**O**) trail running alongside a low concrete-block wall on the left, where the sign reads *'TENO ALTO'*. Head up between sagging stone walls. You will follow this well marked, lush green trail all the way to Teno Alto. In the first 20 minutes you cross both a track and the Teno road. Closer to the pass, the path is very steep and slippery. Your view commands the entire valley.

You reach a PASS on the **Cumbres de Baracán** (**❶**; **40min**) and enter the hidden valleys of Teno — a completely different world, bleak and rugged. You're at about 800m/2600ft here; the highest point of this great mass is Montaña Baracán at 1003m/3290ft, not far away on the left. (For a better all-round view pop up to the road above.)

The now-shady path continues straight on over the pass, below the road. In a couple of minutes you meet the road again, on a bend: cross over the track branching off the road, to pick up the continuation of the path. A FINGERPOST for the PR TF 57 reassures you. As you round the hillside, a short stretch of path may prove vertiginous for some. Around 15 minutes later, bear right along the crest and begin to

descend into a valley (**1h10min**). After climbing a neatly-paved section of path on the far side of the valley, you round a bend and soon find yourselves on a concrete track above a small farm building. Follow this track for seven minutes, ignoring faint off-shoots, then take the wide cobbled path off to the right (just where the track swings left). You meet the Teno Alto road again several minutes uphill and cross it, passing a SHRINE dedicated to San Jerónimo on your right. Soon your curiosity is satisfied: you rejoin the road and head left into **Teno Alto** (❷; **1h40min**).

To make for Teno Bajo, keep straight ahead across the junction/plaza, on the **PR TF 51** signposted 'PUNTA DE TENO'). You cross a slight crest and descend into another valley. Within 10 minutes you reach another crest and a JUNCTION, where there is a house with shutters on the right. Continue to the right, straight over the crest and then downhill, ignoring a track off to the right. The road now reverts to track. Barely 10 minutes down, you round a bend and come to a junction. Your way is downhill, to the right, signposted 'LA CUEVA' ❸). A few minutes later you meet a road. Just beyond it, follow a faint path down to the left, on the edge of the **Barranco de las Cuevas**. The path becomes clearer further along. For the first stretch, stay to the left of the road, following the edge of the *barranco* downhill. A 5cm/2in diameter WATER PIPE is beside you. On reaching the road again, above a few buildings, follow it to your NEXT TURN-OFF (❹): this comes up some 20m/yds below a house on a bend, just before the road veers right. (The yappy dogs here will alert you!) Here you pick up the path again, descending to the left (some people may find this stretch vertiginous). Keep following the WATER PIPE. You head down the hillside, at times quite close to the edge of the ravine. A tired rock

Opposite: the lighthouse at Punta de Teno; right: Barranco de las Cuevas (top) and old mural at Teno Alto

wall is on your right, and you pass several abandoned stone buildings. Some metres/yards *before* the last of the dwellings in the valley, fork left down another path, quickly reaching the bed of the *barranco*. Here you join a TRACK (**5**; **2h35min**) and follow it to the left.

As you leave the ravine, go right at a fork and, soon after, go through a GATE (please leave it closed as requested). Along this part of the track, more of the coastal tongue comes into view, where dark lava shades meet the royal-blue sea. Fifteen minutes beyond the last houses, the track comes to a dead end, high above the plain. A wall of rock here, **Roque Chiñaco** (**6**), serves as a good windbreak. This is an excellent viewpoint and lunch spot: to the right, the jagged ravine cuts back into the mountainside; to the left is the subdued coastline's only landmark: the lighthouse, sitting on a promontory of black lava. Flickering below you are greenhouses for tomatoes. On clear days La Gomera is visible — its mountains rise very clearly out of the sea, and the two humps of La Palma stand out over to the right.

Your path continues behind the windbreak to a viewpoint, then veers left. Zigzag down the sheer escarpment. Loose rocks and gravel make it very slow going, so enjoy the superb descent *in pauses, not while on the move!* Your only landmark on this stretch is a small covered WATER TANK (**7**), about 25 minutes downhill. The path ends at the left of some large sheds at **Teno Bajo** (**8**; **3h35min**). Opposite is an enormous farm ...

and a windfarm. From here it's an easy hour's stroll to the lighthouse *(faro)* and back. Or you could walk just over 100m to the right and take the hourly 369 bus to the lighthouse and back to Buenavista.

The main walk now heads east on the TF445, enjoying spectacular coastal scenery. Some 50 minutes along, you pass Punta del Fraile, from where there are magnificent views out over the banana groves surrounding Buenavista — and over the coastal path north of the golf course followed in the Short walk. Once in **Buenavista**, keep ahead past Plaza San Sebastián (on your right), to reach the BUS STATION on your left (**9**; **5h30min**).

Walk 21: LOS SILOS • TALAVERA • LOS SILOS

See also photo on pages 110-111
Distance: 12.3km/7.6mi; 5h15min
Grade: ●! very strenuous, with ascents/descents of 850m/2790ft overall. You must be sure-footed and have a head for heights. *Only suitable in fine settled weather.* Various PR trails (see text)
Equipment: walking boots, sunhat, warm fleece, rain-/windproof, suncream, picnic, plenty of water
Transport: 🚐 363 from Puerto to/from Los Silos (Timetable 6); journey time 1h15min, or 🚗 to/from Los Silos car park west of the bus stop(28° 21.886'N, 16° 49.043'W).
Short walk: Los Silos — Talavera — El Palmar: 6km/3.7mi; 2h 35min. ● Strenuous, with a steep ascent of 700m/2300ft; equipment and access as above; return to Buenavista on 🚐 366 (Timetable 11), then 🚐 363 as above. Follow the main walk to ❸ (the 2h05min-point), then refer to the map to descend right to El Palmar along the **PR TF 52.1** and **PR TF 55**, eventually joining the end of Walk 17. Turn left in front of the pharmacy at **El Palmar**, to the TF436. The BUS STOP (🅐) is 100m/yds to the left, on the near side of the road.

High in the hills behind Los Silos we come upon abandoned hamlets and small groves of pines. We edge a ravine with gushing water, hidden deep in the hills, the likes of which you won't find anywhere else on Tenerife. And on the return we follow stretches of a centuries-old manicured path. This walk is tough but, if you allow a whole day, it's manageable.

Get off the bus at the junction of Calle Susana and the bypass road in **Los Silos** (🅾), just south of the CHURCH PLAZA. **Start out** by continuing west along the bypass road for 200m/yds then, 70m/yds before a roundabout, turn left on a road signposted 'PINA/TALAVERA', the **PR TF 55**. The hike takes you up the valley ahead, mostly along the right-hand wall. Ascending past banana and citrus groves, you cross a *barranco* (**10min**) and then take a path climbing to the right — making for a chapel on the hillside above. The hillside is matted with *tabaiba*, asphodels, lavender, prickly pear, *verode, lengua de gato,* and *Aeoniums*.

Within the next 10 minutes you pass the CHAPEL (❶), set on an (enclosed) *canal*. Thick-armed *candelabra* appear, and the path is splashed with purple-flowering *Vitrium*. Los Silos lies below at the foot of a volcanic mound, swallowed up by banana groves. Closer to Talavera, you come into the pine zone, and the sheer-sided valley below closes into a narrow defile. Tierra del Trigo is the village set high in the hills two barrancos away.

Mounting a bouldery crest, you come upon the sad remains of a crumbled hamlet — **Talavera** (❷; **1h25min**). This pretty spot looks out over pine groves. In spring the top of the crest is carpeted in flowers. Leaving the hamlet, keep it to your right, then bear right, to ascend the ridge behind the hamlet. Now you're in cloud territory, on the edge of the laurel forest. Cushions of moss coat the rocks. Some 25 minutes above Talavera, you have an unimpeded view of the El Palmar Valley,

Canary bellflower (Campanula canariensis)

Aeonium nobile

etched from top to bottom in terracing. Yellowy-brown Canary bell flowers flourish here; this creeper is prolific in the forest in spring.

Five minutes along the narrow rocky ridge, you come to a prominent upthrust of rock with a cave-like hollow in it. A steep winding descent into the El Palmar Valley follows, in the thick of the laurel woods. Not far past the big rock, ignore a turn-off to the right signposted for 'EL PALMAR' (**3**; **2h05min**); keep left here on the **PR TF 52.1**. *(But for the Short walk, head right and follow the yellow/white waymarked PR TF 52.1 and PR TF 55 into El Palmar.)*

A steep slippery ascent brings you out onto a track a good 15 minutes uphill (ignore the path forking off left just before the track). Continuing ahead, you meet the main ERJOS/EL PALMAR TRACK (**4**; **PR TF 52**; **2h30min**) cutting across your way, and you follow it to the left for the next 20 minutes.

Just before leaving the valley, you come to your turn-off on the left — a track signposted for 'LAS MORADAS' but marked with an 'X' (**5**; **2h55min**). There is usually a barrier across this track. On the descent, there is a good view back, across to the ridge you ascended. Twenty-five minutes down the

128 Landscapes of Tenerife (Cañadas • Orotava • Teno • Anaga)

track, keep an eye out for your turn-off path; it comes up just beyond a bend, and is signposted 'LAS MORADAS' (**6**; **PR TF 54**; **3h25min**). A brief steep descent follows, before the path veers left round the hillside. (Ignore the faint fork off to the right barely

Some 30 minutes below the abandoned path to the Galería Las Moradas, you pass a lone ruin at Moradas de Arriba, where a rocky outcrop provides the perfect viewpoint down over the banana plantations of Los Silos.

Walk 21: Los Silos circuit via Talavera 129

Senecio sp.

Codeso
(Adenocarpus foliolosus)

Margarita
(Argyranthemum)

Valo
(Plocama pendula)

Sea fennel
(Crithmum latifolium)

two minutes downhill.)

A few minutes downhill, you pass an overgrown path on the right. It used to be quite an adventure to follow this vertiginous path down into the bowels of the *barranco* we have been edging, the **Barranco de Cochinos**, to the Galería las Moradas (see notes about *galerías* on page 44) but now, unfortunately, the path is closed.

Continue past the *galería* turn-off, keeping straight ahead, still on the PR TF 54. This path will take you all the way back to Los Silos; there are no turn-offs. You follow some magnificent sections of old path (see opposite), and the scenery is tremendous.

Some 30 minutes down, you pass a

Taginaste
(Echium decaisnei)

Cerrajón
(Sonchus ortunoi)

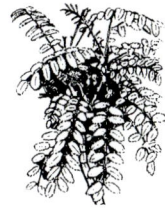

Palo sangre
(Sonchus tectifolius)

Retama
(Spartocytisus supranubius)

Peorera
(Andryala cheiranthifolia)

lone ruin at **Moradas de Arriba** (**7**), where a rocky outcrop makes the perfect viewpoint. Not long after, you pass another derelict outpost, **Moradas de Abajo** (**8**).

Now descending the **Barranco de Bucarón**, the path meets a concrete lane on the outskirts of **Los Silos** (**5h05min**). A few minutes down the lane, a road cuts in front of you. Turn left, quickly reaching the bypass road at its junction with Calle Susana. The BUS STOP (**9**) is just here, where you started out (**5h15min**).

Walk 22: PUNTA DEL HIDALGO • BATAN DE ABAJO • BEJIA • PUNTA DEL HIDALGO

See also the photo on page 133; see the map on the reverse of the fold-out touring map
Distance: 11.7km/7.3mi; 5h
Grade: ● ! strenuous; a steep ascent of 650m/2130ft, much of the way up a path in a river bed (not waymarked). A few vertiginous stretches demand a head for heights. PR TF 11 to return
Equipment: walking boots, sunhat, suncream, light fleece, rain-/windproof, picnic, plenty of water
Transport: 🚌 102/103 from Puerto to/from La Laguna (Timetable 1); journey time 35min; *change to* 🚌 105 to/from Punta del Hidalgo (Timetable 13); journey time 40min. Or 🚗: park at the *mirador* (28° 34.280'N, 16° 19.071'W)

Short walks
1 Punta del Hidalgo — Batán de Abajo: 4.7km/2.9mi; 2h30min. ● ! Grade, equipment and access as main walk (ascent of 550m/1800ft); return from Batán de Abajo to La Laguna on 🚌 274 (Timetable 21). Follow the walk to **Batán** (❸).

2 Batán de Abajo — Bejía — Punta de Hidalgo: 7km/4.4mi; 2h30min. ● ! Moderate, with an overall descent of 650m/2130ft and one vertiginous stretch; equipment/return as main walk; access via 🚌 274 from La Laguna to Batán de Abajo (Timetable 21). Follow the main walk from **Batán** (❸; the 2h30min-point).

This circuit used to be the most challenging hike in the book — along two watercourses hacked out of the sheer rock walls of the valley. These *canals* are still there, forging their way through the wilderness... but they are now off bounds because there have been several hikers' deaths. So if you have an old guide and you try to walk the *canals,* you will find your way blocked. *Do* please think of the grim job the island rescue services have had either helping injured walkers or recovering their bodies from the depths of these *barrancos.*

The walk is still challenging, as you make your way up the Barranco del Río and an 'alpine' ridge to Batán — a

Playa de los Troches, with a view focussing on the Roque Dos Hermanos

Walk 22: Circuit from Punta del Hidalgo via Batán and Bejia

truly off the beaten track village and therefore little changed by tourism. It's very special. I hate to say it again but (as I say in every walk), it's my favourite village.

By the way, while you can see the trails in the Anaga on the map mentioned on page 41, I strongly recommend that you call in at the Cruz del Carmen Information Centre, to see if any trails you are planning to walk require authorisation and, if so, fill in the forms there and then.

Start the walk at the **Punta del Hidalgo** *mirador* (〇). Follow the concrete lane below the viewpoint down to the right (**PR TF 10** signposting 'CHINAMADA' and 'LAS CARBONERAS'). In a couple of minutes, with the beach falling away below you on the left, you pass large greenhouses. The surface changes to gravel underfoot. Continue straight downhill. Soon the track ends, just before a rocky promontory. Continue down a concrete lane behind a chain barrier, descending steeply into the *barranco*. The twin peaks of the Roque Dos Hermanos (the Two Brothers, shown below and on page 133) rise up ahead. Typical coastal, salt-resistant vegetation accompanies you: *tabaiba*, *verode* and *Aeoniums*. You pass a DERELICT BUILDING and, just after, find yourself in the mouth of the **Barranco del Río** (❶). Go right uphill (a left goes to Playa de los

Troches), then fork right, staying in the bed of the *barranco*. You will ascend the path in the stream bed for the next 55 minutes. You have to keep your eyes open to spot the best path, but you can't get lost in the lush confines of this *barranco*.

At the point where a CONCRETE-ENCASED PIPE runs across the *barranco* like a dam (❷; **1h**) and a derelict WATERHOUSE is to the right, you have almost risen to the level of the *canal*. A minute along, you cross the *canal* at its SOURCE. Then you cross to the other side of the *barranco* and ascend the nose of a rocky ridge (by a CAIRN on the right). An 'alpine' path now becomes your way: carved out of the rock, it seems at times to hang in mid air. Higher up the valley you find vineyards terracing the sheer hillsides.

Meeting a junction signposted 'PUNTA HIDALGO', around 50 minutes up from the floor of the *barranco*, bear left. Just after, your way swings left across terraced vineyards. A good five minutes further up, a spectacular view awaits you: mounting a ridge (Picnic 22), you look out over an immense valley sprinkled with little white houses tucked away in the sheer escarpments. In the background is the island's forested backbone, the *cumbre*.

Here you turn right. A couple of minutes later, you round a bend ... to see Batán straight ahead — only a crest away. This small huddle of houses clings to the nose of the ridge above a terraced hillside. It's love at first sight! Keep round the hillside to the village. Ignore all the paths off to plots. The dogs announce your arrival in **Batán de Abajo** (❸; **2h30min**). The village square, with an fine view, is down to the left. The friendly BAR (closed Tuesdays) is opposite the BUS STOP, at the end of the road into the village.

Then, making for Bejía, head straight up the steps from the square (**PR TF 11**). A few minutes up, turn right (by a large WATER TAP and PICNIC TABLES). Your path climbs straight up and over the ridge. Chinamada (Walk 23) is a few houses snuggled into the top of the ridge on the far right. A couple of rooftops introduce Bejía, still a ridge away. Passing over the crest, ignore paths off to the left and right. You head along a cultivated shelf high on a sheer *barranco* wall ... another vertiginous stretch (some handrails).

Twenty minutes from Batán you meet a ROAD and follow it to the right, passing **Bejía** (❹; **2h55min**) — just a few houses set amidst terraced garden plots on a rocky ridge. Some 300m/yds along the road, past two deep bends, watch for a waymark on the left pointing out your ongoing path. At a path junction, turn right, then go down steep stone steps. But just *before* reaching the end of the road (by a house), turn left with the waymarked path. Now it rises and falls gently, dipping into several tributaries of the **Barranco Seco** over to the right.

When you come to a PYLON (❺), a track comes underfoot and you begin the descent, with views to the sea and the attractive lighthouse at the point. The track soon becomes a tarred road. At a T-JUNCTION WITH A 'STOP' SIGN, I suggest you go right, direct to the *mirador* and BUS STOP at **Punta del Hidalgo** (**5h**). Or follow the PR TF 11 straight ahead (left), to reach the TF13 road just to the right of the CHURCH and another BUS STOP.

Walk 23: PUNTA DEL HIDALGO • CHINAMADA • LAS CARBONERAS

See also photo on pages 130-131 and map on reverse of the fold-out touring map
Distance: 7km/4.3mi; 2h 45min (plus optional detour of 25min to the Mirador Aguaide
Grade: ● ! strenuous climb (700m/2300ft overall); possibility of vertigo; partly on PR TF 10
Equipment: walking boots, fleece, rain-/windproof, sunhat, picnic, water
Transport: 🚌 102/103 from Puerto to/from La Laguna (Timetable 1); journey time 35min; *change to* 🚌 105 to Punta del Hidalgo (Timetable 13); journey time 40min. Return on 🚌 275 from Las Carboneras to La Laguna (Timetable 17); journey time 1h05min; *change to* 🚌 102/103 to Puerto (as above)
Alternative walk: Las Carboneras — Chinamada — Las Carboneras: 6km/3.7mi; 2h. ● Easy-moderate, with ups and downs of about 300m/1000ft. Access as for Walk 24, page 136; return by the same buses. From the BUS STOP (**7**) at Las Carboneras, walk back out of the village for four minutes (350m/yds). Then, after the road bends to the left, ascend a path to the right (**c**; which *may be* signposted 'LAS ESCALERAS'). You'll pass a *fuente* (spring) and then come to the **Escaleras** *mirador*, at a junction (**d**; 25min; Picnic 23b). PR TF 10 comes in here. Keep right at the junction. When the path forks, head uphill to the right.

The Barranco del Río, below the twin peaks of the Roque Dos Hermanos

The path rounds a HOUSE (**e**) around 10 minutes up from the junction; ignore the path descending to the left here. Approaching **Chinamada**, ignore a faint path striking off to the right. Minutes later, on reaching the road (1h15min), turn right on the **PR TF 10.1** for **Las Carboneras**, 45min away — or first visit the **Mirador Aguaide**, a 25-minute detour (see the notes for the main walk at the 2h-point at **5**).

Our starting point, Punta del Hidalgo, sits at the end of a steep ridge running down to the coast from the heights of the Anaga range. Get off the bus at the *mirador* just past the village, above the mouth of Barranco del Río. The valley looks impassable from here, as it rises steeply into sharp-edged ridges. Playa de los Troches (Picnic 23a), a rocky beach, is partially hidden by the cliffs below. All this comes as an abrupt change from the market garden plains of La Laguna and the rolling meadows of Tegueste, a wide, sloping valley passed on our descent to Punta del Hidalgo. Chinamada, a tiny, sprinkled hamlet, will delight you with its cave dwellings.

Start the walk by following **Walk 22** to the mouth of the **Barranco del Río** (**1**). After about 30m/yds, fork left, to begin ascending this *barranco* on a path cut into the bank. Above the *barranco* you skirt a thick stone wall. As you begin your (sometimes vertiginous) ascent, great arms of *cardón*, growing out of the slope, will leave you astonished at their size. Purple flowers enrich the setting too — especially the sea fennel (see page 129), which begins flowering in January. Caves of varying sizes and shapes scar the ridge.

Forty minutes up, take care to keep left at a faint fork off to the right. A further 20 minutes up, you come to a LOOK-OUT POINT (**2**) with superb views towards sharp, abrupt ridges dropping down to the sea. Another VIEWPOINT (**3**) follows, as the path briefly makes its way along the edge of the cliffs, where you will hear and see birds darting about. Then, once again, you head back into the valley.

Soon you will notice a distinct change in the vegetation. *Asphodelus*, with its long, thin green leaves and flowers, covers the slope, with the help of grass. A few terraced plots dig back into the inclines. A GRASSY HILL (**4**), hanging off the top of a ridge, is a good spot for surveying the valley below and the banana palms engulfing Punta del Hidalgo. From here on, the way becomes steeper, with steps cut into the edge of the ridge. (If you like, at you *could* soon follow the PR TF 10 up left at **a** to the Mirador Aguaide at **b** and then down to Chinamada. But I prefer the path direct from the village, at **5**.)

Chinamada: like the Guanches, many of these country folk have made their homes in caves nestled in the rocky faces of the ridge.

Walk 23: Punta del Hidalgo • Chinamada • Las Carboneras

Sheer, narrow valleys segment the range. Farmers have terraced the slightest ease in the mountainsides, from the summits down. On rounding a bend, neat stepped plots announce the beginnings of Chinamada. You'll probably reach for your camera at once, to capture on film the houses snuggled into the mountainside. Stone-terraced gardens sit below them. Just beyond these dwellings, you meet a road behind the PLAZA in **Chinamada** (❺; **2h**). There is a bar here, but it is closed Mondays and Tuesdays.

(I highly recommend a 25 minute detour to the Mirador Aguaide from behind this plaza. Climbing above an inhabited cave dwelling, the path circles the left wall of this enclosed valley, where strips of terracing cascade down the hillsides. Further on, you pass a row of abandoned caves and ascend a ridge. Ten minutes from the plaza, you round the hillside to descend to the *mirador* at ❻ — a balcony hanging over precipitous cliffs, from where you have a spectacular view of the island plunging into the sea and over to Punta del Hidalgo in the west.)

But the main walk makes straight for Las Carboneras, following the **PR TF 10.1** all the way. Beyond Chinamada's plaza, fresh meadows, full of clover, roll off the slopes. The mountaintops in front of you are now covered in trees and heather. Heading out of the village, you spot the lovely little white house shown opposite, protruding out of the side of the ridge on your left. A minute further uphill, another house lies over to the right. (The Alternative walk descends the driveway of this latter house.) Climbing out of the valley, you pass a BASIC PICNIC SITE (❻) with tables and benches by the side of the road.

Fifteen minutes uphill, the road cuts through a ridge, affording a spectacular view as you cross another crest. The long deep Barranco de Taborno runs far below. A finely-etched ridge rises up from this valley, leaving only the highest elevations of the Anaga in view. The Roque de Taborno (Walk 24) thrusts its peak above the rest of this razor-edge, while Taborno itself, a handful of white dwellings, straddles the crest midway along.

From the viewpoint follow the road for another 25 minutes, before you arrive at **Las Carboneras**, an attractive mixture of old and new houses, resting on a cultivated hillock extending into the valley. The BUS STOP (❼; **2h45min**) is at the village entrance, by the CHURCH.

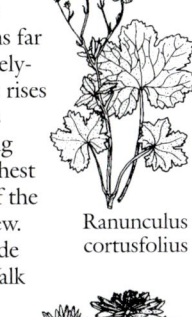

Verode (Rubia tasaigo)

Ranunculus cortusfolius

Red-flowering tabaiba (Euphorbia atropurpurea)

Vinagrera (Rumex lunaria)

Walk 24: LAS CARBONERAS • TABORNO • ROQUE DE TABORNO • CASA CARLOS

Map on reverse of touring map; see also photos on pages 34-35 and 146
Distance: 8/5km/5.3mi; 3h25min
Grade: ●! strenuous, with ascents of about 700m/2300ft overall; *the main walk is recommended for experienced, sure-footed walkers only;* danger of vertigo along the ridge beyond Taborno. Partly PR TF 9, PR TF 2
Equipment: walking boots, fleece, rain-/windproof, sunhat, whistle, water, picnic (or eat at Casa Carlos; their barbecued meat is very tasty)
Transport: 🚌 102/103 from Puerto to La Laguna (Timetable 1); journey time 35min; *change to* 🚌 275 to Las Carboneras (Timetable 17); journey time 40 minutes. Or 🚗 (28° 33.226'N, 16° 16.618'W), in combination with Timetable 17. Return on same buses.

Alternative walk: Las Carboneras — base of Roque de Taborno — Casa Carlos: 7km/4.3mi; 3h. ●
Grade as above, but without the vertiginous and potentially dangerous circuit of the rock. Access/return, equipment as above. Follow the main walk to **Taborno** (**❶**) and on to **❹** (1h30min), then return to the 1h20min-point at **❸**. From there pick up the main walk again at the 2h10min-mark, to reach **Casa Carlos** and the nearby BUS STOP (**❾**).

View from Roque de Taborno to the 'upheaval of pinnacles in the east'

Walk 24: Las Carboneras • Roque de Taborno • Casa Carlos

We enjoy our first view of Roque de Taborno when the bus emerges from the wooded slopes on its descent to Las Carboneras. This perfectly-shaped 'spike' (see page 146) is a prominent feature of the Anaga's landscape of razor-sharp crests. Our hike circles the base of this great sculpture. From a *mirador* on the north side of the rock, a wealth of coastal scenery lies before us. The small pockets of fertile, stepped slopes sitting far out of reach give us some idea of how valuable this arable land once was.

Start out at the BUS STOP in **Las Carboneras** (❶). Head back out of the village, the way the bus came, for 150m/yds. Then leave the road opposite the Bar Valentin, taking the tarred lane heading down into the *barranco* on your left. After 70m/yds, just below house No 2, turn right down concrete steps signposted 'TABORNO' (**PR TF 9**). Now a partly overgrown, but still clear path takes you down grassy slopes. Ignore two paths off to the left and round the hillside, always remaining on the widest path, since many paths branch off to plots.

Around 25 minutes downhill, you cross the stream bed in the **Barranco de Taborno**. On the very steep ascent up the other side, ignore any side-paths. On coming to some fields (**45min**), ignore a turn-off to the right. When you reach the TF138 (**50min**), turn left and follow it into **Taborno** (❶; **1h**). The square rises strategically atop the high thin ridge partitioning the Barranco de Taborno and the Barranco Afur de Tamadiste. This widely-dispersed village could undoubtedly claim to have the best views on the island.

Facing the small CHAPEL in the square, head up the ramp at the right of it. Half a minute up, veer right. Three minutes along, when this wide, red-hued walkway forks, bear right (don't go up the steps).

All the houses here are tiny and well glued to the top of the ridge. Little gardens hug their bases, and prickly pear and aloes surround the lot. Follow the now-narrower walkway until it forks (at the bottom of some steps). The hike will continue to the left, down through a small open copse. But before heading on, don't miss the **Mirador Fuente del Lomo** (❷) down to the right, with its excellent views down into the Afur Valley and the tucked-away village of Afur (Walk 25; photo on page 141).

Then head down through the copse on concrete steps. At the next fork (just after crossing a narrow ridge of rock), swing right on an earthen path. Head towards a SMALL HOUSE, the last in the village, and pass above it (❸; **1h20min**). On rounding the nose of a ridge, you enjoy superb views: Playa de Tamadiste is seen at the mouth of the *barranco* far below on your right, and the two Roques de Anaga sit off the shore. Just after this viewpoint you pass through a GATE, closing it behind you.

Soon the ridge narrows, and you continue along the crest. The walls of the Barranco de Taborno, 'veined' with dykes, are quite spectacular from here. Horizontal strips of smooth green mark the patches of cultivation along the slopes of the ridge. Three minutes

After rounding the Roque de Taborno for about 10 minutes, you climb steeply up to the right — to enjoy this magnificent view.

along this neck of land, the path forks: head left uphill.

On reaching the TOP OF THE RIDGE (④; **1h30min**; Picnic 24), enjoy the view, then turn right and continue around the side of the slope. A minute along, you pass below a small STONE HUT/GOAT PEN (⑤), built into the rock on the crest above. You are now near the base of the rock, which looks less impressive from this angle. *(The Alternative walk turns back here.)*

To begin circling the **Roque de Taborno** clockwise, head down to the left (GREEN WAYMARKS). No turn-offs are necessary, so ignore the paths off to the left some minutes along. After about 10 minutes' walking round the rock (just past a small rock slide and round the end of a small ridge), the route changes abruptly. *Don't continue past the plots ahead: climb steeply up the ridge just to the right* (⑥). Your target is the rock: head up to it, over rocks and along goats' paths. On nearing the rock, 138

continue round to the left, to a PLATEAU VIEWPOINT (⑦) — those who suffer from vertigo may find this stretch unnerving. Ahead, razor-sharp peaks along the coastline fall into the sea, and Almáciga (Walk 28; photo on page 24) is a cluster of white, lost in the upheaval of pinnacles to the east.

As you continue round, directly beneath the rock, the beautiful Afur Valley opens up. Further along, you come to the remains of another GOATS' PEN/CAVE (⑧). Cross through it, to pick up the path — which seems to disappears off the hillside. *Cautiously* make your way round the side of the rock; this vertiginous stretch takes about half a minute. This goats' path leads you back to the FIRST GOATS' PEN (⑤), but now *above* it. Here you clamber down to your original path and retrace your steps to the HOUSE at ③ (**2h10min**). Just past this house, climb down the right-hand side of the ridge and join a path below, high up in the precipitous, winding Barranco de Taborno. Always keep left and uphill, back to the centre of **Taborno** (①; **2h20min**).

Leaving Taborno, ascend the stone ramp on the left, the **PR TF 2** (two minutes out of the village, just past the ELECTRICITY TRANSFORMER building). This path takes you up to the crest of the ridge. After 15 minutes you meet the outward route of Walk 25. Stay on the top of this ridge *(always keeping to the wide, clear PR TF 2 trail)* and huff and puff your way up to **Casa Carlos**. The BUS STOP (⑨; **3h25min**) is at the junction two minutes up the TF12 road.

Walk 25: CASA CARLOS • AFUR • PLAYA DE TAMADISTE • AFUR • ROQUE NEGRO • TF12

Map on reverse of the fold-out touring map; see also photos on pages 26-27, 34-35, 146, 147
Distance: 14km/8.7mi; 6h
Grade: ●❗ very strenuous, *skiddy* descent of 900m/3000ft and ascent of 800m/2600ft; you must be sure-footed and have a head for heights; PR TF 2, 9 and then 8
Equipment: walking boots, sunhat, fleece, rain-/windproof, whistle, picnic, water
Transport: 🚌 102/103 from Puerto to La Laguna (Timetable 1); journey time 35min; *change to* 🚌 275 to Casa Carlos (Timetable 17); journey time 25min. Or by 🚗 (28° 32.331'N, 16° 16.031'W) in combination with Timetable 18. Return on 🚌 76 from Roque Negro to Casa Carlos or La Laguna (Timetable 18); journey time about 50min, or 🚌 077 from the Roque Negro turn-off to La Laguna (Timetable 19); journey time 45min; *change to* 🚌 102/103 to Puerto (as above)

Short walks

1 Casa Carlos — Taborno — Casa Carlos: 7km/4.3mi; 2h15min. ● Moderate descent/ascent of 400m/1300ft. Equipment and access as above; return on the same bus (or 🚗 to/from **Casa Carlos**, as above). Follow the main walk to ❷ (50min); then, instead of going right, head left and follow the road to Taborno. At **Taborno** pick up **Walk 24** at the 2h20min-point (page 138, opposite), to get back to **Casa Carlos**.

2 Afur — Playa de Tamadiste — Taganana: ●❗ 7.4km/4.6mi; 2h30min. Moderate descent/ascent of 250m/820ft, with some stretches of *skiddy and vertiginous path;* equipment as main walk; access on 🚌 102 (as above); *change to* 🚌 076 for Afur (Timetable 18); journey time 1h; return on 🚌 946 from Taganana (Timetable 14); journey time 45min. Follow the main walk from **Afur** (❺) to **Playa de Tamadiste** (❻; 1h). *Don't swim here!* To continue to Taganana, head back to the last stream crossing, a minute back, and ascend the PATH OFF LEFT (ⓐ) that climbs above a big rock. This path takes you all the way to Taganana without any turn-offs. You pass below a farm shed built into a large boulder (1h35min) and reach a spectacular viewpoint, where you join a TRACK (ⓑ; 1h50min). Remain on this track, passing a HAMLET (ⓒ) in 15 minutes and ignoring a road climbing to the right a few minutes later. Then meet a road above **Taganana**: the PR TF 8 turns right here, but after 50m/yds heads left downhill on a lane between the houses. Follow it to the right, into the village. Then find the BUS STOP on the main road behind the CHURCH (2h30min).

Winter is often wet, but the Afur Valley is at its best then. The main stream carries enough water to hold pools big enough for a dip. Summer reduces the stream to a weary trickle. The days are hot, and the landscape burns under the strong sun as the fresh green flora fade. The views on our descent open up the dim corners of this rugged landscape, and the sound of cascading water accompanies us for much of the way. The tough ascent is eased by a couple of bars…

The walk begins at **Casa Carlos** (**⓿**), just downhill from Cruce Las Carboneras, where you leave the bus. Take the signposted lane running downhill, on the right-hand side of the restaurant PR TF 2). A minute down, pass to the left of another house. Here the track becomes a wide path *(very slippery when wet)*, as it slides down the ridge. In less than five minutes ignore forks both to the left and right. A minute later, you find yourselves above a small weekend cottage secured to the top of the ridge, overlooking the **Afur Valley**.

At **27min** you leave this ridge and descend the **PR TF 2.1** (**❶**) trail on your right. You zigzag down the hillside, then briefly ascend to the left, to an adjoining ridge overlooking the **Barranco de Guarda**. Your route (now the **PR TF 9**) continues along the crest of the ridge, with uninterrupted vistas of Taborno and Roque Negro, the black, monumental mound of rock rising up out of the landscape on your right. A small white village of the same name nestles slightly below it.

You meet the TABORNO ROAD (**❷**) at **50min**. *(The Short walk keeps left here.)* Cross the road and, just below it, come to a WATER TAP on the right. Some buildings stand over to the left, and a stupendous panorama lies before you: Playa de Tamadiste (your next landfall), the far ridges that rise and fall as they head seaward, and Roque Negro. From the water tap, continue down over the ridge to the right (still PR TF 9). On the descent, hamlets and solitary houses appear out of nowhere. Two minutes down, you pass beside the cave dwellings shown on page 147. The path brushes to the left of them and falls away to the valley floor. A signposted path joins you from the right and another path joins from the left within the next 10 minutes. Soon a most beautiful sight appears — an intimate cluster of white cottages, **Afur de Arriba** (**❸**), hedged in behind prickly pear, cuddling a crest of rock. From here a wide concrete walkway comes underfoot. You pass just below this hamlet. Ignore a track to the left and continue downhill on concrete, then swing over to the left side of the ridge and continue on down to the stream. Afur, lodged in a swollen ridge of rock, is seen at its best from this approach. A BRIDGE carries you across the stream (**❹**; **1h30min**). After another crossing, a minute later, you climb to **Afur** (**❺**), where there is a friendly bar (just past the CHAPEL).

To make for the beach, follow the concrete path past the bar — the signposted **PR TF 8**. This becomes a path by the last house in the village and turns right. In about five minutes you cross a track coming from the parking area and come upon a FINGER OF ROCK at the left of the path. Starting the descent, you find yourselves not far above the **Barranco Afur de Tamadiste** and small cultivated plots.

About 10 minutes from Afur, at the end of a ridge (by a LARGE BALANCING ROCK), turn sharp right to continue on the PR TF 8. It rises at first but, two minutes along, it descends steep gravelly rock and concrete steps. This steep descent is protected by wooden handrails (mentally reassuring for vertigo sufferers, *but don't lean on them!*). From the next crest, another steep descent takes you down to the stream, where a dyke slices across the landscape and the

Walk 25: Casa Carlos • Afur • Playa de Tamadiste • TF12   141

barranco. You go through the DYKE and come to a scenic spot in the gorge, just beyond the stream crossing. From here steps take you part of the way up the rocky embankment. A good 10 minutes later, the beach comes into view. On passing through a neat terraced vineyard in another two minutes, keep right, down to the valley

View down over Afur from the water tap near the road to Taborno

Inside the simple church at Afur, with Christmas flowers

floor. The path now follows the stream bed (over loose stones) all the way to **Playa de Tamadiste** (❻; **2h30min**). En route you pass a couple of beautiful rock pools. The stony beach is flanked by sheer high cliffs. It's an ideal spot for solitude ... except for weekends. *But swimming here is suicidal!*

The 1h30min return along the same clear path is straightforward. Back in **Afur** (❺; **4h**), head up past the CHAPEL, then descend the path on the right, just behind the tall electricity building (the path on which you arrived). A couple of minutes down, cross the first bridge below Afur, then turn left immediately. Continue up to the houses above, soon passing an appealing house. A couple of minutes past it, at a junction, turn right. A minute later, just above a street lamp, the path swings up left to climb the hillside. Ignore a path to the right, to two houses, then veer right above these houses, towards a TV antenna on the hillside not far ahead.

You round the hillside into the **Barranco del Agua**. Ignoring faint goat paths, you now begin a noticeable ascent. Fifteen minutes uphill, from the top of a ridge, you look straight onto a sheer rock face clinging to the ridge, where the little WHITE CAVE HOUSES shown on pages 42-43 sit precariously on a thin ledge. It's quite a picture — two steps out of the front door, and you'd tumble into the gorge. From this pass, head up to the right. Another path joins you from the left about eight minutes past the house, and a second one comes from the right a few minutes later.

Some 50 minutes up from Afur you pass several houses and come onto a small road which takes you up to the TF136 (❼; **4h50min**) and the STOP FOR BUS 076 (recommended for motorists returning to Casa Carlos). The enormous 'Black Rock' for which the village is named surges up before you here. Walk into **Roque Negro** (❽), then continue up the road for 20-25 minutes. Just after a sharp bend, past a BUS SHELTER, climb a lovely shady path on the left, signposted 'DEGOLLADA DE LAS HIJAS'. It leads to the main TF12 road. A BUS STOP (❾; **6h**) is 100m/yds to the right, opposite a bar/café.

Walk 26: PICO DEL INGLES • BARRANCO DE TAHODIO • SANTA CRUZ

Map on reverse of the fold-out touring map
Distance: 9km/5.6mi; 2h50min
Grade: ● moderate descent of 1000m/3300ft; initially PR TF 2
Equipment: walking boots, fleece, windproof, sunhat, picnic, water
Transport: 🚌 102/103 from Puerto to La Laguna (Timetable 1); journey time 35min; *change to* 🚌 275, 076, 077 or 273 (Timetables 17-20); journey time 30min. Ask for 'Pico del Inglés'; buses stop at the turn-off to this viewpoint (only bus 273 goes to the viewpoint itself). Return on 🚌 945, 946, 947 or 910 from Avenida de Anaga to the intercambiador, then 🚌 100/102/103 from Santa Cruz to Puerto

Mirador Pico del Inglés is the magnificent starting point for this walk. From this *mirador* we look out east to the mass of valleys cutting up the Anaga Peninsula, and west to El Teide and the plains of La Laguna and La Esperanza. We also have a preview of our route immediately below on the right. The best time of year to do this walk is in winter, when small waterfalls and rock pools fill the bed of the Tahodio *barranco;* in summer the lower reaches are dry.

From the BUS STOP, head straight along to the *mirador* — some 10 minutes from the TF12. After enjoying the views, walk down the steps to the left of the *mirador,* from where you will follow the white/yellow marked **PR TF 2**, signed to 'VALLESECO' (**О**). **Start the walk here:** the path is flanked by tree heather; it takes you round the back of the building. Ignore all paths off to the left, including a trail signed to 'Degollada de las Hijas' (**5min**).

Come to a RUINED STONE HOUSE on the right (**15min**). A minute later, ignore a small path to the left. Two minutes further on, at **Cuatro Caminos** ('Four Roads'; **❶**), keep to the middle route along the ridge. Soon, from the TOP OF A CREST (**❷**; Picnic 26) you have views down into the valleys on either side. A dark, MUDDY DAM can be seen in the valley floor — the Presa de Tahodio, shown overleaf. Several minutes later you can take a path off left to a viewpoint on the **Cabezo del Viento** (**❸**).

Past here you start to descend: parts of Santa Cruz appear and, beyond it, the inclines of La Esperanza. El Teide, the island's masterpiece, rises impressively in the background. The nose of a ridge supplies the perfect viewpoint. Five minutes later, ignore a path striking off left.

Around **45min** into the hike, you pass **Los Berros** (**❹**) — an old farmstead high on the slopes. You *leave* the PR TF 2 here: it turns off left here, just past the highest house; keep *right,* past the THRESHING FLOOR on your left. Soon, approaching another house, you encounter two turn-offs two minutes apart: go right at the first and left at the second, passing below the house. Then go right downhill at the junction for 'BARRIO DE LA ALEGRIA' (**❺**).

Shortly after, you cross the bed of the narrow **Barranco de Valle Luis.** Remaining on the right-hand side of this *barranco,* you pass below two more deserted houses a minute later. Skirt a very small, dry

144 Landscapes of Tenerife (Cañadas • Orotava • Teno • Anaga)

DAM (**6**; **1h30min**) on the left, from which a *canal* veers off round the slope to the right. Just past the dam, ignore a path to the right: keep left, through abandoned fields. You recross the main stream twice in fairly quick succession, then pass some neat plots on your right — almond, fig and loquat trees make this a pleasant spot. One more stream crossing takes you past a farm shed, where chained dogs may go beserk! The *barranco* has meanwhile narrowed quite considerably.

Cross the stream bed twice more, ignore a fork off to the left, and then meet a ROAD (**7**; **2h05min**). Follow this road down the **Barranco de Tahodio**, all the way to the Avenida de Anaga. The BUS STOP for the centre of **Santa Cruz** (**8**; **2h50min**) lies a couple of minutes along to the right.

The Presa de Tahodio is seen from the top of a crest early in the walk.

Walk 27: TAGANANA • AFUR • TABORNO • LAS CARBONERAS

Map on reverse of touring map; see also photos on pages 26-27, 141, 142
Distance: 9.2km/5.7mi; 4h35min
Grade: ● strenuous, with steep ascents (900m/3000ft overall) and descents (500m/1650ft overall). PR TF 8, PR TF 9
Equipment: walking boots, sunhat, fleece, rain-/windproof, water, picnic
Transport: 🚌 100/102/103 from Puerto to Santa Cruz (Timetable 1); journey time under 1h; *change to* 🚌 946 to Taganana (Timetable 14); journey time 45min. Return on 🚌 275 from Las Carboneras to La Laguna (Timetable 17); journey time 1h05min; *change* to 🚌 100/102/103 to Puerto (as above)

Short walks
1 Taganana — La Cumbrecita — Taganana: 4.5km/2.8mi; 1h40min. ● Strenuous ascent/descent of under 400m/1300ft; equipment and access as above; return on the same bus (or 🚗 to/from Taganana: 28° 33.540'N, 16° 12.988'W). Follow the main walk to ❸ (1h) and return the same way.
2 Casa Forestal de Anaga — Taganana: 3.5km/2mi; 1h40min. ● Moderate, with a steep descent of 600m/1970ft *(dangerous if wet)*; equipment as main walk, access by 🚌 077 (Timetable 19) from La Laguna to the *casa forestal*, beyond La Cumbrilla; journey time 45min; return on 🚌 946 from Taganana to Santa Cruz (Timetable 14); journey time 40min. Start out on the track running past the left-hand side of the red-painted FORESTRY HOUSE/ POLICE STATION, then take the path forking right off this track, the **PR TF 8**, signposted 'TAGANANA'. A couple of minutes uphill, at a cave, ignore a fork off right. Minutes later, pass a turn-off to the left and begin the steep descent into the **Barranco de la Iglesia**. Less than 50 minutes down, leave the forest to descend amidst plots, ignoring a fork off to the right three minutes later. At 1h15min meet the AFUR/ TAGANANA JUNCTION (❷), and descend to right. On coming to the ROAD (❶), bear left and, two minutes later, on a sharp bend, descend a concrete lane to the right (Camino Portugal). Rejoining the road, go right. When you reach the CHURCH in **Taganana**, walk to the right of it, then take the first left, to the TF134. The BUS STOP (○) is opposite.

Discovering the rural depths of the Anaga involves high ascents over long lateral ridges and descents into deep, shady valleys. Here's your chance to meet the locals as they work their fields and collect fodder for their animals. Break up this rather long walk with a refueling stop at the amiable bar in Afur. It's my favourite: the owner still has time for tourists and hikers. Short walk 2 follows the magnificent old path from the *cumbre* to Taganana, a serpentine descent (the 'Vueltas de Taganana') down the face of a sheer escarpment, in the depths of the cool, damp, moss-laden laurel wood.

View to Roque de Taborno on the approach to Las Carboneras

Taganana is a beautiful farming village with cobbled streets and typical Canarian dwellings. Your bus stop is the second in the valley. The BUS SHELTER (🅾), where **the walk starts**, is in a parking bay. Cross the road and follow the narrow tarred road up into the village. Within a minute, ignore a lane off to the right. Turn left here and then go right immediately, rounding the CHURCH. In half a minute, at another junction, turn left. Here's your chance to capture some good photos of rural life: arms of closely-knit houses extend down and across the slope. Palms, loquats, dragon trees and orange trees adorn individual gardens.

After crossing a small bridge, the road continues up the hillside, but you do not. Beyond the bridge (**5min**), take the second left turn up a narrow street (Camino Portugal) which soon becomes a wide cobbled path. A few minutes of winding up between beautiful old houses brings you onto the road again, where you head left. Two minutes up the road, turn right on a cobbled path (❶; **PR TF 8** to 'AFUR'); it skirts the right-hand side of a *barranco*, where the last houses of the village huddle together.

On coming to a FORK (❷; **25min**), go right, *leaving* the PR TF 8 (there *may* be a sign for 'AFUR'). The path rises to a track, where you turn left uphill. After 100m/yds, at a fork, keep left on a cobbled track, and after another 100m take the small flight of steps on the right, on to a DONKEY TRACK. Keep straight uphill past freshly-tilled land, much of it vineyards that produce Taganana's *vino rosado*. Higher up on the grassy slopes, the bleating of goats echoes across the hills. The path narrows,

Walk 27: Taganana • Afur • Taborno • Las Carboneras

and slowly the slopes close out Taganana. The only landmark on this unsigned path will be a mass of large boulders covered with grey lichen, running down the slope on the left.

On coming to **La Cumbrecita**, a PASS south of Roque el Fraile (**❸**; **1h**), you overlook two very different valleys: the Taganana is a large valley, with sharp outlines and enormous salients of rock jutting out of the landscape, while the Afur Valley is a mould of ridges and gullies. Lone dwellings perch on these ridges, above the valleys that slice up the landscape. Roque de Dentro rises out of the sea far in the background, over on the Taganana side of the ridge. *(Short walk 1 turns back here.)*

To head on to Afur, keep right and downhill on an earthen path. Ignore a path turning off to the right a minute down; then ignore all further forks. Sheltered by inconsistent patches of tree heather, this path takes you down to the first habitations, 15 minutes below the crest. Here you cross straight over a CONCRETE LANE. Meeting the lane again, follow it steeply down for five minutes, then leave it by heading right to a FARM, from where a trail takes you down to the AFUR ROAD (**❹**). Turn right. After about 10 minutes, the PR TF 8 joins the road and leaves it to the left after about 100m/yds. Follow this concrete walkway into the centre of **Afur** (**❺**; **1h45min**) — just a bar/shop, a few modest houses, and a pretty little church.

Your continuation to Taborno starts just behind the TALL ELECTRICITY SUBSTATION that you passed on your way down into Afur, just before the little church. *(You are following Walk 25, but in reverse, so the waypoint numbers below refer to*

This group of houses, concealed in the rock below the local 'laundry', comes as a surprise on the path between Afur and Taborno (Walks 25 and 27).

that walk.) Follow this path (**PR TF 9** for 'TABORNO') down to a confluence of streams, an ideal picnic spot. There are few places on Tenerife where the water flows so abundantly, and even this source dries to a trickle in high summer. A small concrete bridge takes you over the first stream, from where you bear right to a second stream crossing a minute later. Cascading water pours into an already-overflowing pool.

Taganana's 16th-century church of Nuestra Señora de las Nieves, fronted by an Indian laurel, is one of the oldest on the island.

Once over the SECOND BRIDGE (❹), head up the ridge; don't bear right. *Asphodelus,* with its long, thin, blade-like leaves and white-flowering stalks, covers the slope, along with scatterings of purple *Senecio*. The view back to Afur from here shows its superb setting, as the great wall of rock plays guardian to the little houses in its niches. When the path forks, just below a hamlet (**Afur de Arriba**; ❸), keep to the left of the ridge. Rock walls, a deep mauve in colour, and untamed clumps of prickly-pear cactus prevent you from catching more than a fleeting glimpse of the individual houses. Ignore the faint fork off to the left not far above the houses (there *may* be a sign for 'TABORNO' here); then keep right all the way up.

You may be surprised to come upon yet another group of houses, shown on page 147. Concealed from the rest of the valley, they are set back safely into the side of the ridge. The path brushes past them. From above them, you have a superb outlook: the view catches all the small dwellings sheltering behind rocky ridges and in corners of the valley. Roque Negro, a solid mass of black rock rising up from the slopes and encircled by trees at its base, stands out well, slightly to your right. A minute later, by a WATER TAP (❷) on the crest, you enjoy views down to the beach. This is the local laundry spot. The two farmhouses, a little below you to the left, are the last of the solitary homes before Taborno.

Leaving the PR TF 9, make for the road above the houses and follow it into **Taborno** (❶; **3h30min**). Red-flowering aloes cheer your approach to the large, open square, from where there are tremendous views across the razor-sharp ridges.

Las Carboneras is now just over on the next ridge. To get there, follow the road out of Taborno. The Carboneras path (again the **PR TF 9**) leaves the road at a gap in the roadside barrier 425m/yds (10 minutes) past the ELECTRICITY SUBSTATION/STONE RAMP where Walk 24 turns off. A minute downhill, this steeply-descending path passes the remains of an old SHRINE embedded in the slope on the left, assuring you it's the correct route. Just down from the shrine, the path forks. Keep left and head towards the garden plots. The bottom of the *barranco* is where you are heading, so ignore all turn-offs.

Around 15 minutes off the road you cross a trickle of water running down the *barranco*. From here on, it's a steady climb (ignore all turn-offs) past plots and grassy slopes. On reaching the TF145, the BUS STOP is to your right, just where you enter **Las Carboneras** (**4h35min**).

Walk 28: EL BAILADERO • CHINOBRE • CABEZO DEL TEJO • EL DRAGUILLO • ROQUE DE LAS BODEGAS

Map on reverse of the fold-out touring map; see photos on pages 24-25 and 28
NB: A permit is needed to walk in the protected Pijaral area (including the main and both Alternative walks, but *not* the Short walk). The application is only in Spanish on the government website (centralreservas.tenerife.es/ actividad/1), despite the fact that the website has English pages. So either email them in advance *in English:* medionatural@tenerife.es, or telephone 00 34 901 501 901/ 922 633 576. They will want to know your name, address, email address, what day you wish to visit, time of day you plan arrive/leave, and the number in your group.
Distance: 12km/7.4mi; 4h20min
Grade: ● moderate ascent of 300m/1000ft, followed by a steep descent of 800m/2600ft; the paths are slippery when wet
Equipment: walking boots, fleece, rain-/windproof, whistle, picnic, water
Transport: 🚌 100/102/103 from Puerto to Santa Cruz (Timetable 1); journey time 1h; *change to* 🚌 946 (Timetable 14); journey time 45min. Leave the bus at the 'El Tunel' bus stop (just before the tunnel). Or by 🚌 in combination with Timetable 14. Return on 🚌 946 from Roque de las Bodegas to Santa Cruz (Timetable 14); journey time 55min; *change to* 🚌 100/102/103 to Puerto (as above)

Short walk: Benijo — El Draguillo — Benijo: 4km/2.5mi; 1h15min.
● Easy climb of 100m/300ft; equipment as above, but stout shoes will suffice; access by 🚌 to/from Benijo (28° 34.443'N, 16° 11.269'W). Use the map on the reverse of the touring map to reach **El Draguillo** by track and return the same way. **PR TF 6.2**

Alternative walks
1 El Bailadero — Chinobre — Cabezo del Tejo — Chamorga: 7.5km/4.6mi; 3h. ● Moderate; ascent of 300m/1000ft and descent of 400m/1300ft; equipment/access as main walk; return on 🚌 947 from Chamorga to Santa Cruz (16.30, 19.25 (19.55 weekends)). Follow the main walk to the El Draguillo turn-off (**7**), then head right to **Chamorga**, 30min away (keep left at the junction met en route). **PR TF 6, PR TF 7**
2 Chinobre circuit: ● 6.3km/4mi; 2h25min. Moderate; ascent/ descent of 300m/1000ft; the trails can be slippery when wet. Equipment as main walk. Access by 🚌 (28° 33.374'N, 16° 10.790'W) or 🚌 247 to KM.4.8 on the TF123 — *request stop:* ask for 'La Ensillada'. Follow the main walk from **3** (1h15min-point) via the **Chinobre** junction (**4**) to the **Cabezo del Tejo** (**6**). Then take the track here back to the TF123. Turn right on the road and right again almost at once (**c**), on a rising path which takes you back to **b** in under 15 minutes. Turn left, back to **La Ensillada**.

From the port city of Santa Cruz our journey takes us to the dramatic northern coast and its isolated villages. In between, high-forested mountain trails rise and fall over moss-cushioned crests. Remains of the original laurel forests darken and roof our way. But unsurpassed views lie at regular intervals along this spine of the Anaga range.

El Draguillo

Your bus stop is just before a road tunnel that takes the TF134 into the Taganana Valley. Although you've bought a ticket for El Bailadero, reaching this *mirador* involves a 15-minute hike. **The path begins** just across the road from the PARKING AREA/BUS STOP (**O**). Keep right at the junction under 10 minutes up. Reaching the TF123 at **El Bailadero** (**❶**), turn right. (But if you first want to go to the famous viewpoint, you will have to walk past the hideous pistachio-coloured buildings to the left...) Quickly passing an attractive walkers' hostel, follow this road for the next half hour; then, 100m/yds short of the KM2 ROAD MARKER, climb rough steps off left (**❷**; **45min**), heading into the trees. Almáciga is glimpsed far below. Go left at a fork some 10 minutes up the path. Then keep to the main path, ignoring all turn-offs left downhill. This area is called the **Pijaral** — named for the many ferns growing among the laurels. It is now under protection: they want to limit walkers to 45 a day.

Rejoining the road, head left downhill. Five minutes along, 200m/yds short of the KM5 ROAD MARKER, turn left on a wide path blocked to traffic by BOLLARDS (**❸**; **1h15min**). (This used to be a picnic site called 'La Ensillada' and is still known by that name, but there are *no longer any signs here* — although there *are* usually several parked cars.) About 20 minutes along this path, a turn-off left (**❹**; **1h40min**) leads to the **Chinobre** *mirador*, a rocky nodule three minutes uphill (909m/ 2980ft). It was *closed to walkers at press date, however, even those with a permit.* At the Cruz del Carmen Visitors' Centre they were unable to say when it would reopen. If you *can* turn left, you will come to one of the best viewpoints on the whole island, equalled only by Teide and Guajara. The views encompass El Teide, Santa Cruz, San Andrés, Taganana, Taborno and Almáciga. Multitudes of ridges dissect the backbone of the Anaga into narrow isolated valleys.

Back on the main path, turn left. (Or just keep straight on if you have not been able to get to the viewpoint.) A minute downhill, ignore a fork to the right. You're now walking in the setting shown on pages 24-25. A further 30 minutes brings you face-to-face with a large projection of rock towering above the trees.

This bare-faced rock is called **Anambra** (**5**), and it makes another good viewpoint over the hidden northern valleys. The **Cabezo del Tejo** (**6**; **2h20min**) is yet another magnificent lookout, with panoramas to the west. *(Alternative walk 2 follows the track from here to the TF123 — generally easy going, but awkward when wet.)*

The main walk continues on the steeply descending path at the end of this viewpoint. Reaching an intersection, turn left on the **PR TF 6** for 'EL DRAGUILLO' (**7**). *(But for Alternative walk 1 keep right.)* Once you emerge from the trees, El Draguillo discloses itself sitting back on the sea-cliffs. From here the village is a tight bunch of dulled rooftops, smothered in prickly pear. Forty minutes down from the junction, ignore the PR TF 6.3 turning off to the left. At just over **3h20min** you meet the 'king' of dragon trees outside **El Draguillo** (**8**). It is, of course, for this DRAGON TREE that the village was named. But 'El Draguillo' means the *little* dragon tree, and it certainly has grown in the intervening years! Let's hope that all the names and initials carved into its trunk don't kill it off!

Below the tree, ignore the PR TF 6 off right to Las Palmas. Follow the track, then road to the left, beside stunning coastal scenery (Picnic 28), to the seafront BUS STOP in **Roque de las Bodegas** (**9**; **4h20min**).

Walk 29: CHAMORGA • ROQUE BERMEJO • FARO DE ANAGA • TAFADA • CHAMORGA

Map on reverse of touring map
Distance: 7km/4.3mi; 3h35min
Grade: ●❗ strenuous descent/ascent of 600m/1950ft; danger of vertigo. Those who suffer badly from vertigo will find the Tafada return too difficult and should return along the outgoing path. PR TF 6 and PR TF 6.1
Equipment: walking boots, fleece, rain-/windproof, picnic, water, whistle
Transport: 🚌 to/from Chamorga (or 🚌 947 from Santa Cruz to Chamorga at 07.00 or 10.15 *weekends only;* returns 16.30, 19.55)
Short walk: Chamorga — Tafada — Chamorga: 4.5km/2.6mi; 1h 55min. ●❗ Moderate, with an ascent of 250m/820ft, but as vertiginous as the main walk; equipment, access as main walk. Start out on the path across from the CHURCH (**PR TF 6/7**). Ignore a fork to the right at the outset. After about 10 minutes, follow the trail round to the left (*not* the path straight ahead up the *barranco*). Your trail bends back right and climbs the left-hand side of the *barranco*. Three minutes later, ignore a left turn for Cumbrilla. In another 20 minutes turn right at the CABEZO DEL TEJO/EL DRAGUILLO JUNCTION (**❼**). Five minutes later, after stunning cliff-top views, ignore a path descending to right. Keep left all the way along the ridgetop to **Tafada** (**❻**; 1h20min) — a derelict building. Now follow the main walk from the 3h-point to **Chamorga**, 35 minutes away.

Alternative walk: Chamorga — Roque Bermejo — Faro de Anaga — El Draguillo — Roque de las Bodegas: 13km/8mi; 5h20min.
●❗ Strenuous, with overall ascents of 400m/1300ft and descents of 950m/3100ft; you must be surefooted and have a head for heights; danger of vertigo; equipment, access *by bus* as main walk; return on 🚌 946 from Roque de las Bodegas (as Walk 28, page 149). This walk, somewhat easier than the main hike, visits some of the most spectacular scenery on Tenerife. Follow the main walk to the LIGHTHOUSE (**❹**) and then the turn-off above it (**❺**; 2h10min), where it leaves the main path to head up a crest to Tafada. Instead, keep straight along the main path (**PR TF 6**). Ten minutes from the turn-off, come to a pleasant picnic spot, by a SPRING (**ⓐ**). Coming to an enormous rock with cave dwelling and a wine press on the top (**ⓑ**; **Las Orobalas**), circle it to the right, then bear left to cross the *barranco* (please close the gate after you). Ascending, you pass below **Las Palmas** (**ⓒ**; 3h10min) and head along the sea-cliffs. A stiff ascent takes you up and across steep hillsides, covered in loose gravel, before you descend to **El Draguillo** (**❽**; 4h; photo pages 150-151). From here take the track to **Benijo**, then the TF134 to **Roque de las Bodegas** (**❾**), 1h10min away (see notes for Walk 28 and photo on page 151).

Chamorga, a serene little village, beautifully sited in the isolated northeastern tip of the island, is where our hike begins and ends. From Chamorga we follow a narrow, shaded ravine that winds its way down to the idyllic bay of Roque Bermejo, only accessible on foot or by boat. An old

Anaga lighthouse (top) and (right): Chamorga, almost opposite the bus stop, steps lead down to a pretty chapel.

lighthouse gives warning of Roque Bermejo — a sharp, reddish crag clinging onto the edge of the island far below. Rocky crests, with clear sea views down grassy slopes, return us to Chamorga.

Begin the walk in the village square at **Chamorga** (**O**). Just north of the church, fork right downhill on a path, the **PR TF 6** for 'ROQUE BERMEJO'. Cane fills the moist valley floor. Five minutes along, you ascend to a track at the point where it narrows into a path. This path leads to the beach, without any turn-offs (although after half an hour you *may* have to deviate steeply down and back up, to round a landslide). A small stream idles its way down the ravine (**Barranco de Roque Bermejo**), replenishing the pools. A view of a faded-white house, set in the V of the *barranco*, is the first landmark as the ravine opens out to the nearby sea (**45min**). This is followed by Roque Bermejo, and shortly after, the lighthouse appears.

You reach a couple of OLD HOUSES (**❶**), joined together, overlooking the small basin shown above. Down in the ravine are tanks of water in store for the long dry summer and curtailing any would-be cascades. The basin, hemmed in by high escarpment walls, is a wealth of produce. To descend past these plots, turn left at the old building and make your way down the steep path. Take a deep breath and enjoy the scent from the Canarian lavender bushes.

A few minutes above Roque Bermejo, at a signposted intersection, turn right for 'BERMEJO' (**❷**; **1h10min**). A few minutes downhill, you come to a small CHAPEL with a well-tended garden, and a large house with a tremendous view down into the bay. A sign indicates that this is the settlement of **Roque Bermejo** (❸). The path at the right of the house leads to a small stony beach; the path between the chapel and the house goes to the port area, where you can swim from the steps of the quay. At the foot of Roque Bermejo sits a well-protected, crystal-clear pool set in the rocks. However, this is only accessible at low tide. The port area offers good bathing, however, for confident swimmers. This beautiful enclosed rocky bay is encircled by the sheer slopes that mark the end of the island.

Back at the JUNCTION (❷), head straight up the wide old lighthouse path, signposted 'EL FARO, LAS PALMAS' (still the PR TF 6). The **Faro de Anaga** (❹), a good 20 minutes uphill, is a pleasant place to recuperate from the steep climb and take in the surroundings.

The continuation of your path clambers over rock, to the left of the lighthouse. On the crest of the ridge, behind the lighthouse, the Roques de Anaga are visible. Five minutes up from the lighthouse (a minute or two up the crest), *leave* the main path and continue up a smaller path on the left (❺; **PR TF 6.1**; **2h10min**), making for the crest above. This path heads straight up the ridge, so you can't go wrong. *(The main PR trail continues to Las Palmas and is the route of the Alternative walk.)* Your route is up the very steep grassy slope; it affords good views over both sides of the lateral ridge as you ascend.

Eventually you leave the crest of the ridge and start moving inland, constantly climbing. As you rapidly gain height, the terrain becomes rockier and more sheer, with the possibility of vertigo for those unaccustomed to heights. Enormous *Aeoniums* plaster the bare rock faces. Heading round into an inner valley, the path passes above a natural balcony of rock — an excellent viewpoint for the Roques de Anaga. Not far above this, the path divides: both forks lead to Tafada. The left fork goes via the top of the crest, with spectacular views. **Tafada** (❻; **3h**), just a solitary stone farm building cradled in a dip in the ridge, makes a good viewing point. From here you look straight down into the Barranco de Roque Bermejo.

Continue up the left-hand side of the ridge, keeping left at the fork. Those who suffer from vertigo will find this path unnerving for a couple of minutes. As you round a crest two minutes later, Chamorga's school — slightly apart from the rest of the village — comes into sight in the distance. At this point, the path begins descending a steep rock face. This is another place where *those prone to vertigo may well find themselves unable to continue.* There's a rickety piece of railing to help, *but don't lean on it!*

Less than 15 minutes from Tafada, you cross a crest and come upon a picture-postcard view of Chamorga (Picnic 29). On the descent, notice the 'dog's head'-rock at the end of this crest. Cumbrilla sits safely across the valley on a parallel ridge. A further 10 minutes down, you reach the first houses and a bar/shop in **Chamorga** (**3h35min**). Before leaving, be sure to sample the superb local wine and goats' cheese.

Walk 30: IGUESTE • BARRANCO DE ZAPATA • PLAYA DE ANTEQUERA • BARRANCO DE ANTEQUERA • IGUESTE

Map on reverse of touring map
Distance: 12km/7.4mi; 5h35min
Grade: ●❗ very strenuous, with total ascents/descents of over 900m/3000ft; you must be sure-footed and have a head for heights; danger of vertigo. *Recommended for experienced/adventurous walkers only.*
Equipment: walking boots, sunhat, fleece, rain-/windproof, walking stick(s), whistle, picnic, plenty of water
Transport: 🚌 100/102/103 from Puerto to/from Santa Cruz (Timetable 1); journey time 1h; *change to* 🚌 945 to/from Igueste (Timetable 15); journey time 30min. Or 🚗 to/from Igueste (28° 31.575'N, 16° 9.256'W)

Short walks
1 Igueste — 'Semáforo' — Igueste: 4.5km/2.8mi; 2h10min.
● Strenuous ascent/descent of 400m/1300ft, but no danger of vertigo; equipment and access as main walk. Follow the main walk to ❶ (55min), then continue to the **Semáforo** (**ⓐ**), the old abandoned tower, for an excellent view over the Playa de Antequera. Return the same way. **PR TF 5.1**
2 TF123 — Las Casillas — Igueste: 5.5km/3.4mi; 2h15min.
● Easy, with a long descent of 600m/1970ft; equipment as main walk; access on 🚌 947 from Santa Cruz (Chamorga bus; departs 07.00/10.15 *(weekends only)*, departs 15.00 daily; ask to be dropped off at 'el camino para Las Casillas'; journey time 1h); return as main walk. The trail (**PR TF 5**) begins where you leave the bus, by a small road to the **Las Bodegas CEMETERY** and a sign for the PR TF 5 to 'IGUESTE' (**ⓑ**). Follow this well-worn path towards Las Casillas, ignoring all forks turning straight uphill or down. You will meet a fork within the first 20 minutes as you ascend to the top of a crest: you can go either way, the strands rebraid. Below the first house encountered, at a fork, climb uphill to the right. **Las Casillas** (**ⓒ**; Picnic 30b) is reached in 30min. From the hamlet, initially veer left round the side of the ridge. Five minutes later the path takes you over the ridge, to descend the right-hand side. Some 15 minutes from Las Casillas, back on the top of the crest, you come to a JUNCTION (**ⓓ**; just beyond the last telephone pole). Head right here for Igueste. Five minutes later you pass a second path off to the left: here descend to the right, joining the main walk which has climbed up from the Playa de Antequera. Pick up the notes for the main walk notes from ❼ on page 158.

Playa de Antequera lies in one of the most beautiful bays on Tenerife. The fact that it is only accessible by boat or on foot makes this tranquil little harbour even more special. The short walks make ideal early-evening excursions. The long bus journey to reach the starting point of Short walk 2 is an adventure in itself: the minibus twists and winds its way up and along the *cumbre* on a ribbon of road, tooting on every corner. If there's a cloudless sky, you'll be rewarded with unsurpassed views. By contrast, it's just a short coastal ride above small, sandy coves set in the cliffs to get to Igueste (de

San Andrés), where the main walk and Short walk 1 begin. This proud little village, with its well-tended groves of mangoes, avocados, guavas and bananas, sits just up from the sea, inside the Barranco de Igueste. Stay on the bus to the end of the road, where the bus turns round.

Start out in **Igueste** by following the paved path (**O**; the white/yellow-waymarked **PR TF 5.1**) off the end of the road to the plaza. Climb the steps behind the CHURCH, then turn left into the first alley (Pasaje Julio). Take the first right turn and then the second left, to pass a tall TV MAST and head towards the CEMETERY. After about 50m/yds go up steps that initially take you to the left, before turning right onto a slowly climbing footpath. Shortly afterwards, turn left on a beautiful old steeply rising path marked with an ARROW. You leave the village behind, heading towards an old tower. This tower ('Semáforo') was used before the days of radio, to send hand-signals. Chiselled out of the slope, the path climbs relentlessly. *Euphorbia,* various cacti, and bright green, drooping *valo,* with its soft, needle-like leaves, cover the hillside. White chrysanthemums are in full bloom in spring. A PROMINENT ROCK, standing just off

Playa de Antequera

Walk 30: Playa de Antequera from Igueste 157

the path (**35min**), makes a good viewpoint over the coastline towards Santa Cruz.

Just before the path levels out, and immediately opposite a 6m/yd-long gap in the low man-made rock wall you have been following, turn left inland (❶; **55min**; CAIRNS). *(But the Short walk continues straight on with the PR TF 5.1 to the signal tower.)* Clamber over a rough, rocky trail to the crest of this ridge. On reaching the crest, continue to the left, to a derelict CHAPEL (❷; **1h15min**). This is a lovely spot to take a break and feed the tame lizards! Igueste lies far below, set above the groves of fruit trees. **Montaña de Atalaya**, on your right, just a couple of minutes away (marked by a white pillar), is the best spot for viewing Playa de Antequera. There's no path to the summit, but the climb is very straightforward.

From the chapel continue along the path, crossing the crest. Ten minutes from the chapel, in the upper reaches of the **Barranco de Zapata**, strike off right towards the beach (❸; **1h30min**). Your turn-off comes just after the path has levelled out; a small CAIRN marks the spot. Descending rapidly, you drop through the remains of old terraced plots into the valley below. The path is amply marked with CAIRNS. You first cross a gully, then scramble down to the riverbed, sometimes on all fours; follow the CAIRNS. At the point where the path you have been following turns sharp right to cross the river bed (it descends to Playa Zapata), look for your path off left, waymarked with CAIRNS (❹; **1h55min**; not always easy to spot).

From here on, you remain on the left side of the *barranco,* gradually ascending. Dark, gaping holes mark the hillsides. *Cardón* (see page 1) adds a touch of severity to the slopes. Another dry stream bed is crossed, then the path climbs again. Keep more or less level round the hillside. You pass a shepherd's shelter — a rocky overhang with the remains of a couple of small STONE PENS. Later the path heads below an impressive DYKE slicing its way seaward down the escarpment. Looking around the sheer hillside, you have a stunning view of the Playa de Antequera. Beyond the dyke, you head up a very steep and narrow goats' path — a vertiginous stretch, high above the sea, with sheer drops to the right. *Tabaiba* (page 135) and more brilliant green *valo* bushes (page 129) cover the slopes.

At the end of the ridge, overlooking the Barranco de Antequera, the path veers off down the nose of the ridge to **Playa de Antequera** (❺; **2h45min**). Two lone dwellings sit in a gentle curve in the slopes above the beach, and a small harbourside building — long since abandoned — lies at the end of it.

Your return is via the **Barranco de Antequera**, directly behind you. Follow the path that climbs to the houses from the building at the harbour. Walk to the left of the FIRST HOUSE and to the right of the SECOND HOUSE. The path briefly follows a large WATER PIPE.

The Barranco de Antequera is every bit as dramatic as the Barranco de Zapata. Green-leafed *tabaiba* and curly-leafed sea fennel (page 129) illuminate the inclines with their brightness. A buttress of rock crowns the top of the ridge above you. Less than 15 minutes

Barranco de Igueste, from the road at the end of the walk

up, you round the nose of a ridge and have a spectacular view back down to the beach framed by the walls of the *barranco*. A few minutes later you cross the *barranco* — the first of many crossings. Your path ascends steadily; the vegetation thickens and soon swallows you up.

Ignore the faint fork off to the left (usually blocked off with stones) just before crossing the *barranco* for the sixth time. The valley has now become lush with greenery and, nearer the pass, large rosetted *Aeoniums*, perfectly circular, are plastered across the rock walls, interspersed with the clinging branches of chunky *candelabra*. Then, just before crossing the pass, you walk below a bare rock face.

Some 1h30min up from the beach you reach the pass, the **Degollada Pasito del Corcho** (**6**; **4h15min**), from where you look straight down into the Barranco de Igueste. The path continues up the crest, heading right, and then forks after about 50m/yds: go half-left here. Descending into the **Barranco de Igueste**, you soon notice the aroma of *Artemisia*, a green/grey-leafed plant. *Attention:* a minute further on, you pass beneath a POWER CABLE. A goats' path continues straight on here, but you scramble *uphill to the right*, across a rocky face with well-worn steps cut into it. This fork takes you onto the **PR TF 5** LAS CASILLAS/IGUESTE PATH (**7**) in three minutes. *(Short walk 2 joins here.)* Here you descend to the left (there may still be a PAINTED STONE MARKER). Ignore a faint fork off to the right about 18 minutes downhill.

Meeting a concrete lane, continue down to the ROAD (**8**; **5h10min**). Turn left and descend to **Igueste** (**5h35min**). There's a BUS STOP where you enter the village, or five minutes along to the left, where the bus turns round.

BUS TIMETABLES

Below is a list of destinations covered by the following pages of timetables, which give access to all the walks in the book. Numbers following place names are **timetable numbers**. There are far more buses *and departures* than those listed here; see the latest TITSA timetables on their interactive website, **titsa.com** (with English version).

Afur 18	El Palmar 11	La Montañeta 8	Pico del Inglés 17-20	Roque de las Bodegas 14
Aguamansa 2, 5	El Portillo 5, 9*	La Montañeta del Palmar 11	Playa de las Américas 9*, 12	Roque Negro 18, 19
Benijos 10	Erjos 7, 16	La Orotava 2, 3, 5, 10	Puerto de la Cruz 1-6, 16	San Juan de la Rambla 6
Buenavista 6, 11	Icod de los Vinos 4, 6, 7, 8, 16	Las Carboneras 17	Punta de Teno: see 'Special touristic route' at the foot of page 161	San José (turn-off) 7
Casa Carlos 17, 18	Icod el Alto 4	Las Portelas 11		Santa Cruz 1, 12-15
Costa Adeje 7, 9, 12	Igueste 15	Los Silos 6		Taborno 17
Cruz de Taganana 18, 19	La Caldera 2	Montaña Blanca 5, 9*		Taganana 14
Cruz del Carmen 17, 18, 19, 20	La Guancha 4	Palo Blanco 10	Punta del Hidalgo 13	Teide cable car 5, 9*
El Bailadero 14	La Laguna 1, 13, 17-20	Parador 5, 9*	Realejo Alto 10	

See page 168 for more information about buses and the tram

1 🚌 100/102/103: Puerto de la Cruz to Santa Cruz

There are currently three basic services between Puerto and the intercambiador in Santa Cruz, the capital, and only one stops at the intercambiador in **La Laguna**.

Bus 100 is a workers' bus, running Mon-Fri *only*, and taking only 35min (a non-stop service). Departs Puerto 08.40, 09.10, 10.25, 11.10, 15.00, 16.15. Departs Santa Cruz 06.50, 09.30, 10.00, 13.20, 13.50, 15.15. This bus uses exit ❺ from Puerto and stops are shown on the plan on pages 8-9.

Bus 102 runs daily and takes 1h, leaving Puerto from Exit ❹. Departs Puerto 06.05 and every 30min until 21.10; departs Santa Cruz 06.25 and every 30min until 21.25. **Calls at La Laguna**

Bus 103 runs daily and takes 45min, leaving Puerto from Exit ❻. Departs Puerto 06.25 and generally every 30min until 21.00; departs Santa Cruz 06.10 and every 30min until 21.40. **Calls at La Laguna**

2 🚌 345: Puerto de la Cruz to La Caldera; daily

Puerto	La Orotava	Aguamansa	La Caldera
08.45	09.00	09.30	09.45
	and every hour at 45 minutes past the hour until		
17.45	18.00	18.30	18.45
La Caldera	**Aguamansa**	**La Orotava**	**Puerto**
09.40	09.45	10.20	10.35
	and every hour at 40 minutes past the hour until		
18.40	18.45	19.20	19.35

3 🚌 352/353: Puerto — Realejos* — Orotava circuit; daily**

Puerto	La Orotava	La Orotava	Puerto
05.30	05.50	06.20	06.45
	and approximately every 20-30min until		
01.00	01.20	02.00	02.25

*The Los Realejos junction/roundabout, where the TF320 crosses the TF5
This is a circular route from the station in Puerto via the **Orotava bus station, stopping at **Las Arenas** (bus 102) and the **Los Realejos junction** (bus 354). The circuit takes 70 minutes. Bus 352 first heads east to La Orotava (about 20min); bus 353 heads west to Los Realejos (also about 20min).

4 🚌 354: Puerto (via Realejos*) to Icod de los Vinos; daily

Puerto	Junction	Icod el Alto	La Guancha	Icod de los Vinos
07.05	07.20	07.55	08.05	08.20
and at least every hour at 35min past the hour until (weekends at 10 or 40 min past)				
21.35	21.50	22.25	22.35	22.50
Icod de los Vinos	**La Guancha**	**Icod el Alto**	**Junction**	**Puerto**
08.05	08.20	08.30	08.45	09.00
and at least every hour at 15min past the hour until (weekends at 10 or 40 min past)				
20.05	20.20	20.30	20.45	21.00

*The Los Realejos junction/roundabout, where the TF320 crosses the TF5

160 Landscapes of Tenerife (Cañadas • Orotava • Teno • Anaga)

5 🚌 348: Puerto de la Cruz to Las Cañadas; daily

Puerto (depart)	09.30	Parador (depart)	16.00
La Orotava	09.45	Teide cable car	16.05
El Portillo	10.30	Montaña Blanca	16.15
Visitors' Centre	10.32	Visitors' Centre	16.28
Montaña Blanca	11.05	El Portillo	16.30
Teide cable car	11.20	La Orotava	17.10
Parador	11.30	Puerto	17.30

6 🚌 363: Puerto de la Cruz to Buenavista; daily

Puerto	San Juan	Icod de los Vinos	Los Silos	Buenavista
06.00	06.20	06.45	07.15	07.20
		and every 10-30 minutes until		
21.30	21.50	22.15	22.45	22.50
Buenavista	Los Silos	Icod de los Vinos	San Juan	Puerto
06.30	06.35	07.05	07.30	07.50
		and every 10-30 minutes until		
22.00*	22.05	22.35*	23.00*	23.20*

*the bus at 20.30 terminates at Icod de los Vinos; all others go through to Puerto

7 🚌 460: Icod de los Vinos to Costa Adeje; daily

Icod	Erjos	San José turn-off	Guía de Isora	Costa Adeje
07.35	08.10	08.15	08.50	09.20
10.00	10.35	10.40	11.15	11.45
11.50	12.25	12.30	13.05	13.35
14.00	14.35	14.40	15.15	15.45
16.10	16.45	16.50	17.25	17.55
18.15	18.50	18.55	19.30	20.00
20.15	20.50	20.55	21.30	22.00
Costa Adeje	Guía de Isora	San José turn-off	Erjos	Icod
07.45	08.15	08.50	08.55	09.30
09.50	10.20	10.55	11.00	11.35
11.55	12.25	13.00	13.05	13.40
14.10	14.40	15.15	15.20	15.55
16.00	16.30	17.05	17.10	17.45
18.25	18.55	19.30	19.35	20.10
20.00	20.30	21.05	21.10	21.45

8 🚌 360: Icod de los Vinos to La Montañeta (Puerto de Erjos bus); daily

Icod	La Montañeta	*La Vega*	La Montañeta	Icod
07.15	07.50		10.10	10.45
09.30	10.05	*lies half-*	12.15	12.50
11.40	12.15	*way between*	15.45	16.20
14.40	15.15	*Icod and*	19.10	19.45
18.30	19.05	*La Montañeta*	—	—

9 🚌 342: Costa Adeje to Las Cañadas; daily

Costa Adeje (depart)	09.25	El Portillo (depart)	15.15
Los Cristianos	09.40	Visitors' Centre	15.20
Arona	09.50	Montaña Blanca	15.30
Vilaflor	10.10	Teide cable car	15.40
Parador	11.10	Parador	16.00
Teide cable car	11.25	Vilaflor	17.00
Montaña Blanca	11.40	Arona	17.20
Visitors' Centre	11.50	Los Cristianos	17.30
El Portillo	11.55	Costa Adeje	17.45

10 🚌 347: La Orotava to Realejo Alto; daily

La Orotava	Benijos	Palo Blanco	Cruz Santa	Realejo Alto
09.00	09.20	09.30	09.40	09.50
11.05	11.25	11.35	11.45	11.55
13.05	13.25	13.35	13.45	13.55
15.05	15.25	15.35	15.45	15.55
17.00	17.20	17.30	17.40	17.50
19.10	19.30	19.40	19.50	20.00
Realejo Alto	**Cruz Santa**	**Palo Blanco**	**Benijos**	**La Orotava**
09.50	10.00	10.10	10.20	10.40
12.05	12.15	12.25	12.35	12.55
14.05	14.15	14.25	14.35	14.55
16.05	16.15	16.25	16.35	16.55
17.50	18.00	18.10	18.20	18.40
20.05	20.15	20.25	20.35	20.55

11 🚌 366/🚌 355: Buenavista to Las Portelas; daily

Buenavista	El Palmar	*Bus 366: Mon to Fri*	El Palmar	Buenavista
07.30	07.45*		07.55#	08.10
09.30	09.45*		09.20#	09.35
13.30	13.45*		14.00#	14.15
18.10	18.25*		16.00#	16.15
19.35	19.50*		18.30#	18.45
Buenavista	**Santiago del Teide**	*Bus 355: Daily*	**Santiago del Teide**	**Buenavista**
09.30	10.25*		11.00+	11.55
12.00	12.55*		13.10+	14.05
15.45	16.40*		17.05+	18.00
17.55	18.50*		19.30+	20.25

*arr La Montañeta 1min and Las Portelas 5min later; #dep Las Portelas 5min earlier/+ approx 20min later

12 🚌 111: Santa Cruz to Costa Adeje; daily

Santa Cruz	Candelaria	Airport	Los Cristianos	Costa Adeje
06.25	06.40	07.15	07.50	07.55
		and every 30minutes until		
20.55	21.10	21.45	22.20	22.25
Costa Adeje	**Los Cristianos**	**Airport**	**Candelaria**	**Santa Cruz**
07.25	07.35	07.55	08.30	08.45
		and every 30minutes until		
21.25	21.35	21.55	22.30	22.45

13 🚌 105: Santa Cruz to Punta del Hidalgo; daily

Santa Cruz	La Laguna	Tegueste	Bajamar	Punta Hidalgo
05.50	06.20	06.35	06.45	07.00
		and every 30min until		
20.15	20.45	21.00	21.10	21.25
Punta Hidalgo	**Bajamar**	**Tegueste**	**La Laguna**	**Santa Cruz**
06.15	06.20	06.35	06.50	07.20
		and every 30min until		
20.15	20.25	20.40	20.55	21.25

'Special touristic route': 🚌 369
Due to the road to Punta de Teno being subject to rockfall, it was often closed to motorists in the past. A few years ago, a bus service was intoduced, starting at Buenavista. The bus runs hourly and takes 20min, but in stormy conditions it will not run. If you are motoring, a handy place to park for the bus is at the barrier on the roadside (see page 30) *if you arrive early enough; parking is limited to about a dozen cars.* The bus leaves Buenavista station (good parking) daily on the hour (or a few minutes past the hour) from 09.00 until 19.00, returns from the point at 25min past the hour from 09.25 until 19.25. Fare-saving tickets are accepted.

162   Landscapes of Tenerife (Cañadas • Orotava • Teno • Anaga)

14 🚐 946: Santa Cruz to Almáciga/Roque de las Bodegas; daily

Santa Cruz	San Andrés	El Bailadero	Taganana	Almáciga
		Mondays to Fridays		
10.30	10.40	11.05	11.15	11.20
13.10	13.20	13.45	13.55	14.00
14.25	14.35	15.00	15.10	15.15
17.15	17.25	17.50	18.00	18.05
		Saturdays, Sundays and holidays		
09.10	09.20	09.45	09.55	10.00
10.55	11.05	11.20	11.30	11.35
12.55	13.05	13.20	13.30	13.35
11.40	11.50	12.15	12.25	12.30
14.15	14.25	14.50	15.00	15.05
17.05	17.15	17.40	17.50	17.55

Almáciga	Taganana	El Bailadero	San Andrés	Santa Cruz
		Mondays to Fridays		
14.20	14.25	14.35	15.00	15.10
15.30	15.35	15.45	16.10	16.20
18.10	18.15	18.25	18.50	19.00
19.25	19.30	19.40	20.05	20.15
		Saturdays, Sundays and holidays		
14.00	14.05	14.15	14.40	14.50
15.30	15.35	15.45	16.10	16.20
18.10	18.15	18.25	18.50	19.00
19.25	19.30	19.40	19.55	20.05

15 🚐 945: Santa Cruz to Igueste; daily

Santa Cruz	Igueste		Igueste	Santa Cruz
07.25	07.55	*Departs from*	09.30+	10.00+
08.40+	09.10+	*San Andrés*	11.30+	12.00+
09.30	10.00	*about 15min*	12.20	12.50
10.40+	11.10+	*from Santa Cruz*	13.30=	14.00=
11.35	12.05	*(outbound)*	15.10	15.40
12.30+	13.00+	*and 15min*	17.10	17.40
14.10	14.40	*from Igueste*	19.10	19.40
16.10	16.40	*(inbound)*	21.10	21.40
18.15	18.45		15.30	16.00

+only on Sat/Sun/holidays; =not on Sat/Sun/holidays

16 🚐 325: Puerto — Icod de los Vinos — Los Gigantes; daily

Puerto	Icod	Los Gigantes	Los Gigantes	Icod	Puerto
09.00*	09.25*	10.45*	08.15	08.45	10.00
10.30	10.55	12.15	11.10*	11.40*	12.55*
15.50	16.25	17.45	12.35	13.05	14.20
18.45*	19.10*	20.30*	18.30	19.00	20.15

*Mon-Fri only; bus calls at Erjos 1h15min from Puerto and 30min from Los Gigantes

17 🚐 275: La Laguna to Las Carboneras and Taborno; daily

		Mondays to Fridays		
La Laguna	Cruz del Carmen	Casa Carlos**	Las Carboneras	Taborno
06.50	07.10	07.15	07.45*	07.30*
09.35	09.55	10.00	10.30*	10.15*
13.15	13.35	13.40	13.55	14.10
15.25	15.45	15.50	16.05	16.20
18.50	19.10	19.15	19.30	19.45
		Sat, Sun/holidays		
07.25	07.45	07.50	08.10	08.25
12.00	12.20	12.25	12.45	13.00
16.05	16.25	16.30	17.00	16.45

*Calls at Taborno before Las Carboneras; **also called Cruce Las Carboneras

Bus timetables

Taborno	Las Carboneras	Casa Carlos**	Cruz del Carmen	La Laguna
07.35	07.50	08.00	08.05	08.30
10.20	10.35	10.45	10.50	11.15
14.15*	14.00*	14.25	14.30	14.55
16.20*	16.05*	16.30	16.35	17.00
19.50*	19.35*	20.00	20.05	20.30
		Sat, Sun/holidays		
13.00*	12.45*	13.15	13.20	13.40
17.00*	16.45*	17.15	17.20	17.40

*Departs Las Carboneras before calling at Taborno; **also called Cruce Las Carboneras

18 🚌 076: La Laguna to Afur and Roque Negro; daily**

La Laguna	Casa Carlos**	Casa Forestal	Roque Negro	Afur
		Mondays to Fridays		
07.00	07.25	07.50	08.05	08.15
13.30	13.55	14.20	14.35	14.45
16.05	16.30	16.55	17.10	17.20
19.00	19.25	19.50	20.05	20.15
		Sat, Sun/holidays		
07.00	07.25	07.50	08.05	08.15
13.15	13.40	14.05	14.20	14.30
16.25	16.50	17.15	17.30	17.50

Afur	Roque Negro	Casa Forestal*	Casa Carlos**	La Laguna
		Mondays to Fridays		
08.00	08.10	08.25	08.50	09.15
14.35	14.45	15.00	15.25	15.50
17.30	17.55	18.10	18.35	19.00
20.00	20.10	20.25***	20.50	21.15
		Sat, Sun/holidays		
08.00	08.10	08.25	08.50	09.15
14.45	14.55	15.10	15.35	16.00
17.45	17.55	18.10	18.35	19.00

*Also called 'Cruz de Taganana'; **also called Cruce Las Carboneras; ***20.00 bus from Afur does not pass

19 🚌 077: La Laguna to El Bailadero*; daily

La Laguna	Pico del Inglés**	Roque Negro**	Casa Forestal	El Bailadero
10.25	10.55	11.10	11.30	11.40
18.00***	18.30	18.45	19.05	19.15

El Bailadero	Casa Forestal	Roque Negro**	Pico del Inglés**	La Laguna
11.30	11.40	12.00	12.15	12.4
19.00****	19.10	19.30	19.45	20.15

*Also called 'Cruz de Taganana'; **turn-off to; ***18.00 Sat, Sun/holidays

20 🚌 273: La Laguna to Pico del Inglés; Sat/Sun/holidays *only*

		Sat, Sun/holidays only		
La Laguna	Pico del Inglés		Pico del Inglés	La Laguna
09.25	09.50		10.00	10.25
11.00	11.25		11.35	12.00

21 🚌 274: La Laguna to Batán de Abajo; daily

La Laguna	Batán		Batán	La Laguna
		Mon-Fri		
07.30	08.10		15.50	16.30
15.05	15.45		18.45	19.25
		Sat, Sun/holidays		
09.05	09.45		09.50	10.30
14.15	14.55		15.00	15.40

Index

Geographical names comprise the only entries in this index. For all other entries, see Contents, page 3. A page number in **bold type** indicates a photograph; a page number in *italic type* indicates a map (both may be in addition to a text reference on the same page. 'TM' refers to the large-scale walking map of the Anaga Peninsula on the reverse of the touring map. See also Bus timetable index, page 159.

Adeje (Ah-**day**-hay) 20, 23
Afur (Ah-**foor**) 17, 26, 139, 140, 141, **142**, 145, **147**, 148, 159, *TM*
Aguamansa (Ah-gwah-**mahn**-sah) 20, *56-7*, 59, *60*, *62*, 65, 69, *70*, 159
Alcalá (Ahl-kah-**lah**) 23
Almáciga (Al-**mah**-see-gah) 25, **28**, *TM*
Anaga Peninsula (Ah-**nah**-gah) 25, **34-5**, 130-158, *TM*
Arafo (Ah-**rah**-foh) *72-3*, 75
Arico (Ah-**ree**-koh) 37
Arona (Ah-**roh**-nah) 24, 159
Bajamar (Bah-hah-**mar**) 34
Barranco (Bah-**rahn**-koh) river, ravine
 Afur de Tamadiste (Ah-**foor** day Tah-mah-**dees**-tay) 140, *TM*
 de Antequera (day Ahn-tay-**kay**-rah) 155, 157, *TM*
 de Bucarón (day Buh-kah-**rohn**) *127*, 129
 de Guarda 140, *TM*
 de Igueste (day Eeg-**west**-tay) 156, **158**, *TM*
 de la Arena 51, *52*
 de la Madre del Agua 64, *65*, **66**, *70*
 de las Cuevas (day lahs Koo-**ay**-vahs) *122-3*, 124, **125**
 de los Llanos (day lohs **Lyah**-nos) 11, *60*, *72-3*, 78
 de Roque Bermejo (day **Roh**-kay Behr-**may**-hoh) 153, *TM*
 de Taborno (day Tah-**bor**-noh) 137, *TM*
 de Tahodio (day Tah-**hoe**-dee-oh) 17, 143, **144**, *TM*
 de Valle Luis (day **Bahl**-yay Loo-is) 143, *TM*
 de Zapata (day Thah-**pah**-tah) 155, *TM*
 del Agua (dayl **Ah**-gwah) **42-3**, *TM*
 del Río (dayl **Ree**-oh) 131, **133**, 134, *TM*
 Seco 132, *TM*

Barranco Ruiz 30, 53, *54-5*, *105*, **106**
Barrio de la Alegría (**Bah**-ree-oh day lah Ah-lay-**gree**-ah) 144, *TM*
Batán de Abajo (Bah-**tan** day Ah-**bah**-hoh) 14, 34, 130, 132, *TM*
Bejía (Bay-**hee**-ah) 130, *TM*
Benijo (Bay-**nee**-hoh) 25, 28, 149, *TM*
Benijos (Bay-**nee**-hohs) *56-7*, 58, 159
Boca Tauce (**Boh**-kah **Too**-say) 22
Buenavista (Boo-ay-nah-**bees**-tah) **14-5**, 30, **114**, 115, *117*, *119*, 121, *122-3*, 125, *127*, 159
Cabezo del Tejo (Kah-**bay**-thoh dayl **Tay**-hoh) 149, 151, *TM*
Café Vista Paraíso 50, 51, *52*
Camino de las Crucitas (Kah-**meen**-oh day lahs Croo-**thee**-tahs)61, 69, *70*
Cañada (plain of sedimentary rock) (Kahn-**yah**-dah)
 Blanca (**Blahn**-kah) *82-3*
 de la Grieta (day lah Gree-**ay**-tah) 80, *82-3*
 de las Pilas (day lahs **Pee**-lahs) 80, *82-3*
 de los Guancheros (day lohs Goo-an-**shay**-rohs) 12, *76-7*, *94*, 95
Canal Vergara (Kah-**nahl** Vair-**gah**-rah) 107, *108-9*, 110
Candelaria (Lah Kahn-day-**lah**-ree-ah) 37, *72-3*, **38-9**
 Candelaria Trail **11**, *72-3*, **74**
Casa Carlos 26, **34-5**, 136, 138, 139, 140, 159, *TM*
Casa Forestal de Anaga 145, *TM*
Chamorga (Shah-**more**-gah) 17, 25, 27, 149, 152, **153**, 154, *TM*
Chanajiga (Shah-nah-**gee**-gah) 12, 56, *94*, 96, 97, *98*, 99
Chinamada (She-nah-**mah**-dah) 16, 36, 133, **134**, 135, *TM*
Chinobre (She-**noh**-bray) 149, 150, *TM*
Chio (**She**-oh) 22

164

Index

Choza (shelter) (**Show**-thah)
  Almadi 64, *65*, 68
  Bermeja *76-7*
  Chimoche (She-**moh**-shay) 11, *56-7*, 59, *60*, 62, *63*, *70*, *72-3*, *76-7*, 78
  Cruz de Fregel (**Crooth** day Fray-**gayl**) *94*, 95
  Cruz de Luis *98*
  El Topo 11, 64, *65*, *70*
  Enrique Talg *98*
  Inge Jua 64, *65*, *70*
  Pedro Gil *60*, **61**, *65*, 69, *70*, *76-7*
  Perez Ventoso (Pay-**rayth** Behn-**toh**-soh) *62*, 64, *65*
  Piedra de los Pastores (Pee-**ay**-drah day lohs Pahs-**toh**-rays) *94*, 96
Corral del Niño (Koh-**rahl** dayl **Neen**-yoh) *76-7*
Costa Adeje 23
Cruz de Hilda *116-7*
Cruz de las Lajitas (**Krooth** day lahs Lah-**hee**-tahs) *65*, 68
Cruz del Carmen (**Krooth** dayl Kahr-**mayn**) 25, 26, 35, 41, 159, *TM*
Cuesta de la Villa (Koo-**ays**-tah day lah **Beel**-yah) 52
Cueva del Hielo (Koo-**ay**-vah dayl Hee-**ay**-loh) *82-3*, 86
Cuevas de los Roques (Koo-**ay**-vahs day lohs **Roh**-kays) *88*, 89
Cuevas Negras, Las (Lahs Koo-**ay**-vahs **Nay**-grahs) *108-9*, 111
Cuevitas de Limón (Koo-ay-**bee**-tahs day Lee-**mohn**) *76-7*
Degollada (pass) (Day-gohl-**yah**-dah)
  de Guajara (day Goo-ah-**hah**-rah) 91, *93*
  de Ucanca (day Oo-**kahn**-kah) *92*, *93*
  del Cedro (dayl **Say**-droh) *94*, 95
  de la Mesa (day lah **May**-sah) 115, *116-7*, 118
El Cabezón (Ayl Kah-bay-**thohn**) *94*, 95
El Draguillo (Ayl Drah-**geel**-yoh) 28, 149, **150-1**, 152, *TM*
El Lagar (Ayl Lah-**gahr**) 13, 100, **101**, *102-3*
El Palmar (Ayl Pahl-**mahr**) 31, **32-3**, **112-3**, *114*, 159
El Pijaral **24-5**, 27, 150, *TM*
El Portillo (Ayl Poor-**teel**-yoh) 12, 20, 37, 38, 41, *76-7*, *82-3*, 84, *94*, 95, **96**, 159
El Rincón (Ayl Reen-**kohn**) 52
El Tanque (Ayl **Tahn**-kay) 33
El Teide (Ayl Tay-**ee**-day) 22, **35**, 43, **58-8**, 67, 78, *82-3*, **84-5**, 87, **88-9**, 159, **cover**
El Turrón 115, *117*
Erjos (**Air**-hohs) 13, 14, 33, 107, *108-9*, 111, 112, *114*, *116-7*, **116-7**, 159
Faro (lighthouse) (**Fah**-roh)
  de Anaga (day Ah-**nah**-gah) 152, **153**, 154, *TM*
  de Teno (day **Tay**-noh) *122-3*, **124**, 125
Fasnia (**Fahs**-nee-ah) 39
Forestal Park 37
Galería (water gallery) (Gah-lay-**ree**-ah) 44
  Chimoche *56-7*, *60*, *70*, *72-3*, *76-7*, 78
  La Fortuita *56-7*, 58
  La Puente *60*, *70*, *72-3*
  La Zarza *94*, 96
  Las Moradas *114*, *127*, **128**
  Pino Soler *56-7*, 58
  Vergara Alta *108-9*, 110
Garachico (Gah-rah-**shee**-koh) 29, 30, **31**, 43
Güímar (Gwee-**mahr**) 37, *38-9*
Icod de los Vinos (**Ee**-kod day lohs **Bee**-nohs) 29, 30, 33, 43, 159
Icod el Alto (**Ee**-kod ayl **Ahl**-toh) 29, 33, *54-5*, 97, *98*, 100, *102-3*, **104**, *105*, 159
Iguestre (Eeg-**west**-tay) 17, 25, 28, 155, 156, 157, **158**, *TM*
La Caldera (Lah Kahl-**day**-rah) 12, 20, *56-7*, 59, *60*, *63*, 64, *65*, 69, *70*, **71**, *72-3*, *76-7*, 78, 159
La Catedral (Lah Kah-tay-**drahl**) *88*, 90
La Cumbrilla (Lah Koom-**breel**-yah) *TM*
La Ensillada 150, *TM*
La Esperanza (Lah Es-pay-**rahn**-thah) 37
La Florida (Lah Floh-**ree**-dah) 62, *63*, 64, *65*, 68
La Fortaleza (Lah For-tah-**lay**-thah) *94*, 95
La Guancha (Lah **Gwan**-shah) 33, 100, *102-3*, 104, *105*, 159
La Laguna (Lah Lah-**goo**-nah) 7, 34, **36-7**, 43, 159
La Montañeta (Lah Mohn-tahn-**yay**-tah) 13, **16**, 107, *108*, 109, *119*

La Orotava, La (Lah Oh-roh-**tah**-bah) 20, 159
La Siete (Lah See-**ay**-tay) 14, 31, *119*, **120-1**
La Tabaiba (pass) (Lah Tah-**bye**-bah) 14, 31, **110-1**, 112, *114*, 115, *117*, *119*
Las Aguas 53, *54-5*
Las Arenas Negras (Lahs Ah-**ray**-nahs **Nay**-grahs) 13, **107**, *108-9*
Las Bodegas (Lahs Boh-**day**-gahs) 155, *TM*
Las Cañadas (Lahs Kahn-**yah**-dahs) 12, 20, **21**, **22-3**, 45, **80-1**, *82-3*, **92-3**, 159
  Parador (Pah-rah-**door**) 22, 43, 79, 81, *82-3*, 91, *93*, 159
  Visitors' Centre *see* El Portillo
Las Canteras (Lahs Kahn-**tay**-rahs) 34
Las Carboneras (Lahs Kahr-boh-**nay**-rahs) 34, 36, 133, 135, 136, 137, 145, **146**, 148, 159, *TM*
Las Casillas (Lahs Kah-**seel**-yahs) 17, 27, 155, *TM*
Las Lagunetas (Lahs Lah-goo-**nay**-tahs) *112*, 114
Las Lajas (Lahs **Lah**-hahs) 20, 24
Las Moradas 112, *114*, *127*, **128**, 129
Las Palmas (Lahs **Pahl**-mahs) *TM*
Las Raices (Lahs Rah-**ee**-thays) 37
Llano de Ucanca (L-yah-noh day Oo-**kahn**-kah) *82-3*, *88*, 90
Lomo de los Brezos (**Loh**-moh day lohs **Bray**-thos) 59, *60*, 69, *70*, *76-7*
Los Bolicos (Lohs Boh-**lee**-kohs) 115, *116-7*, 118
Los Cristianos, *see* Playa de
Los Gigantes (Lohs Jee-**gahn**-tays) 20, 23, 159
Los Hermanos **130-1**, **133**, *TM*
Los Lavaderos 112, *114*
Los Organos (Lohs **Ohr**-gah-nohs) *60*, 69, *70*, 71, *72-3*
Los Partidos de Franquis (Lohs Par-**tee**-dohs day Frahn-**kees**) 107, *108-9*, 111
Los Realejos (Lohs Ray-ahl-**ay**-hohs) 33, *54-5*, *98*, 159
Los Roques de García (Lohs **Roh**-kays day Gahr-**thee**-ah) 12, 22, *82-3*, *88*, **88-9**, **90**, cover
Los Silos (Lohs **See**-lohs) 30, 107, *108-9*, 126, *127*, **128**, 129, 159
Masca (**Mahs**-kah) 31, **32**

Mirador (viewpoint) (Mee-rah-**door**) de Aguaide 16, 133, 134, 135, *TM*
Mirador *(continued)*
  de Baracán (day Bah-rah-**kaan**) 14, 31, **32-3**, *116-7*, *119*, 120
  de Chimague 37
  de Chipeque 37
  de Garachico (day Gah-rah-**shee**-koh) 33
  de Pico Viejo (day **Pee**-koh Bee-**ay**-hoh) 79, *82-3*
  de la Fortaleza (day la For-tah-**lay**-thah) 79, *82-3*
  de la Paz (day lah **Paath**) *8*, 51, *52*
  de la Ruleta (day lah Roo-**lay**-tah) *88*, **90**
  de las Chamucadas (day lahs Sha-moo-**kah**-dahs) 27
  de San Pedro (day Sahn **Pay**-droh) 30, 53, *54-5*
  El Asomadero (Ayl Ah-soh-mah-**day**-roh) 97, *98*
  El Bailadero (Ayl Bye-lah-**day**-roh) 25, **26-7**, 27, 43, 149, 150, 159, *TM*
  El Lance (Ayl **Lahn**-thay) *98*, **104**, *105*
  Fuente del Lomo 137, *TM*
  Jardina (Har-**dee**-nah) **35**
  La Corona (lah Koh-**roh**-nah) 13, 97, *98*, **99**
  La Crucita (Lah Kroo-**thee**-tah) **11**, 12, 37, *58-8*, *72-3*
  Las Escaleras (Lahs Ays-kah-**lay**-rahs) 16, *TM*
  Minas de San José 22, *82-3*
  Montaña Grande 37
  Ortuño (Or-**toon**-yoh) 37
  Pico del Inglés (**Pee**-koh dayl Een-**glays**) 25, 34, 36, 143, 159, *TM*
  Piedra La Rosa (Pee-**ay**-drah lah **Roh**-sah) *56-7*, **57**
Montaña (mountain) (Mohn-**tahn**-yah)
  Baracán (Bah-rah-**kahn**) *116-7*, *119*
  Blanca (**Blahn**-kah) *82-3*, 84, 85, 86, **87**, 159
  de Atalaya (day Ah-tah-**lye**-ah) 157, *TM*
  de Guajara (day Goo-ah-**hah**-rah) **81**, *82-3*, 91, **92-3**, *93*
  de Guamaso (day Goo-ah-**mah**-soh) *76-7*
  de las Arenas (day lahs Ah-**ray**-nahs) **11**, *72-3*
  de Limón (day Lee-**mohn**) *76-7*

Index

de Majuá (day Mah-hoo-**ah**) 79, *82-3*
Jala (**Hah**-lah) 14, 115, *116-7,* 118
Montaña *(continued)*
  Mostaza (Moz-**tah**-thah) 80, *82-3*
  Negra (**Nay**-grah) 107, *108-9,* 110
Montañeta, La (*near* Icod de los Vinos) (Lah Mohn-tahn-**yay**-tah) 13, **16**, 107, *108-9,* 159
  (*near* El Palmar) 112, *114,* 115, *117, 119, 122-3, 127,* 159
Observatorio de Izaña (Ee-**thaan**-yah) 38, *82-3*
Orotava Valley 20, 45, *56-7,* **58-9,** 67, 71
Palo Blanco (**Pah**-loh Blahn-koh) 56, *94,* 96, 97, *98,* **99,** 159
Pico (mountain, peak) (**Pee**-koh)
  Verde *116-7,* 118
  Viejo 79, *82-3,* 87
Piedras Amarillas (Pee-**ay**-drahs Ah-mah-**reel**-yahs) 12, 79, **80,** 81, *82-3,* 91, *93*
Pino Alto (**Pee**-noh **Ahl**-toh) 64, *65,* 68
Pinolere (Pee-noh-**lay**-rees) **62,** *63, 63,* 64, *65*
Playa (beach) (**Ply**-yah)
  de Antequera (day Ahn-tay-**kay**-rah) 155,**156,** 157, *TM*
  de Benijo (day Bay-**nee**-hoh) 17
  de las Teresitas (day lahs Tay-ray-**see**-tahs) **18,** 28
  de los Troches (day lohs **Tro**-shays) 16, **30-1,** *TM*
  de Tamadiste (day Tah-mah-**dees**-tay) 26, 139. 142, *TM*
  del Bollullo (dayl Boh-**you**-yoh) **50-1,** *52*
  de las Arenas **14-5,** *122-3*
Playa de las Américas (day lahs Ah-**may**-ree-kahs) 20, 23, 159
Playa de los Cristianos (day lohs Kreest-**yahn**-ohs) 20, 23
Playa de San Marcos (day Sahn **Mahr**-kohs) 30, 43
Puerto de Erjos (Poo-**er**-to day **Air**-hohs) 14, 33, 115, *117*
Puerto de la Cruz (Poo-**er**-to day lah **Krooth**) **6-7,** 20, 25, 29, 34, 37, 42, 50, 51, *52, 54-5,* 159
town plan 8-9
Puerto de Santiago (Poo-**er**-to day Sahn-tee-**ah**-goh) 23
Punta (point of land) (**Poon**-tah)
  de Teno (day **Tay**-noh) 15, 29, 30, *122-3,* **124**
  del Fraile (dayl **Fry**-lay) 15, 30, *122-3*
  Punta del Hidalgo (**Poon**-tah dayl Hee-**dahl**-goh) 34, **130-1,** 132, 133, 159, *TM*
Rambla, La 13, 53, *54-5,* **106**
Rambla de Castro *54-5*
Ramón Caminero 12
Restaurante Fleytas 14, 107, *108-9,* 115, *116-7*
Roque (rock) (**Roh**-kay)
  Bermejo (Behr-**may**-hoh) 152, 153, 154, *TM*
  Chiñaco *122-3,* 125
  Chinchado *88,* **88-9, cover**
  de Anambra (day Ahn-**am**-brah) 151, *TM*
  de Taborno (day Tah-**bor**-noh) **136, 138,** 146, **147,** *TM*
  del Peral (dayl Pay-**rahl**) *76-7, 82-3, 94,* 95
Roque de las Bodegas (day lahs Boh-**day**-gahs) 28, 149, 151, 152, 159, *TM*
Roque Negro 25, 26, 139, 142, 159, *TM*
San Andrés (Sahn Ahn-**drays**) 25, 28
San José de los Llanos *108-9*
San Juan de la Rambla (San Hu-**an** day lah **Rahm**-blah) 29, 30, 53, *54-5,* **54-5,** *105,* **106**
Santa Cruz (**Sahn**-tah **Crooth**) 7, 43, 144, 159, *TM*
town plan 8-9
Santiago del Teide (Sahn-tee-**ah**-goh dayl Tay-**ee**-day) 29, 31
Taborno (Tah-**bohr**-noh) 16, 34, 36, **136,** 137, 139, 145, 148, 159, *TM*
Tacoronte (Tah-koh-**rohn**-tay) 34
Tafada (Tah-**fah**-dah) 152, 154, *TM*
Taganana (Tah-gah-**nah**-nah) 25, **26-7,** 28, 139, 145, 146, 159, *TM*
Talavera (Tah-lah-**bay**-rah) 126, *127*
Tamaimo (Tah-**my**-moh) 23
Tegueste (Tay-**gwest**-tay) 34
Tejina (Tay-**hee**-hnah) 34
Teno Alto (**Tay**-noh **Ahl**-toh) 29, 31, 115, *117, 119, 122-3,* **125**
Teno Bajo (**Tay**-noh **Bah**-hoh) *122-3,* 125
Vilaflor (Beel-yah-**floor**) 20, 24, 159

SOME BUS AND TRAM INFORMATION

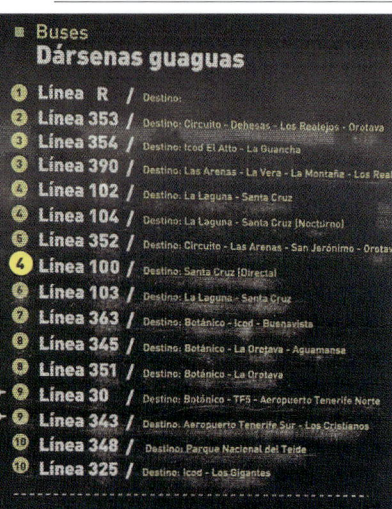

Buses on Tenerife are a dream to use. Just get your tourist ticket for a day or a week and log onto titsa.com's English version to plan your journey. At the left is a photo of the departure board in Puerto; *all bus stations have similar boards.* This tells you the platform *(dársena)* from which your bus will depart and the destinations. At the right (not shown) are 'modules': letters for ticket sales, toilets, food, and other amenities.

The buses themselves are invariably new and comfortable, with USB plugs, seatbelts and information about the next stop *(proxima parada)* on a screen.

Below: buses at Puerto de Erjos

Take Line 1 on the Santa Cruz tram, which starts in front of the intercambiador (bus station). Get off at Padre Anchieta for La Laguna's intercambiador or La Trinidad for the town centre.